EX LIBRIS

MARIO BUATTA

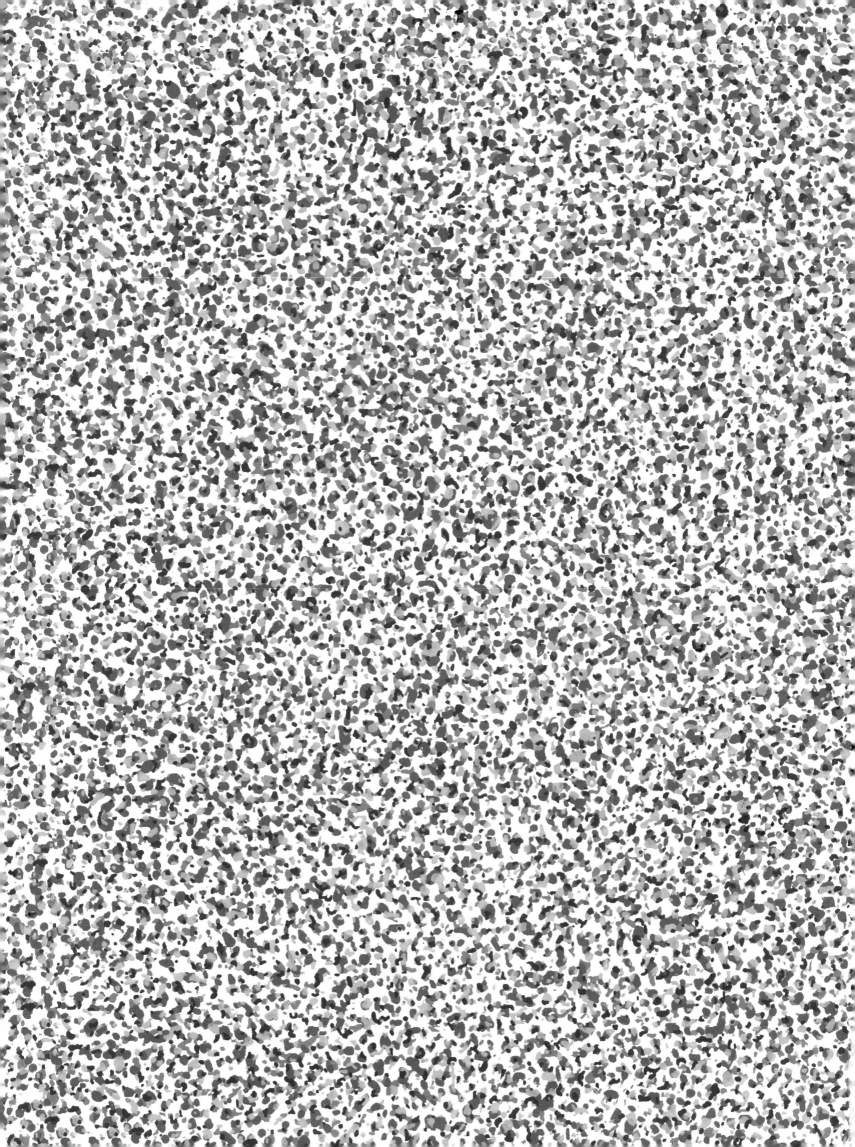

For my Mother and her Sister Mary (who was not a nun).
Their inspiration and support have guided me through my life and career.

MARIO BUATTA

Fifty Years of American Interior Decoration

MARIO BUATTA *with* EMILY EVANS EERDMANS

Foreword by PAIGE RENSE

RIZZOLI
NEW YORK

New York · Paris · London · Milan

The Building

Words by Wendy Wasserstein   Drawn by Blair Drawson

My Dearest Mario Buatta,

My name is Wendy, and I live in Greenwich Village with my cat, Ginger.

My income is stable in the low five figures.

We have so much in common.

I like English chintz, Staffordshire pugs and Edwardian manor houses.

I also love your new decor at 'Blair House.'

Especially since I do some entertaining, too.

I am a reader of 'Architectural Digest,' 'HG' and the Laura Ashley catalog.

And last year I had one shade made from a grape fabric from Clarence House.

Mario, I know that those 25-room Park Avenue apartments must keep you very busy...

but this Valentine's Day my fondest wish is...

that you would arrive at my apartment and be my very own "Prince of Chintz."

CONTENTS

FOREWORD

HE IS A LEGEND. And for good reason. For fifty-some years he has designed extraordinary, traditional interiors combining fine design with shelter, comfort, and joy. His color palette cheers, delights, and offers emotional sustenance. It seems impossible to imagine being depressed in a Mario Buatta interior.

Personally, he also cheers and delights. He is a practical joker. (Look out for gold-plated creepy-crawlies.) He genuinely cares about his clients, who quickly become loyalists. They appreciate his work and his friendship.

When I was editor-in-chief of *Architectural Digest*, it was always a pleasure to show his work, in part because of the fan mail we received from our readers and because a Mario Buatta interior on the cover meant big newsstand sales. He was important to the magazine's success.

Years ago, based in Los Angeles, I went to New York City to meet with major designers, hoping to persuade them to give me their work first. (It was an unwritten law in the field that if a designer showed their work in one so-called shelter magazine, no other magazine would touch it.) Mario was one of the first major designers to believe me about what I said *Architectural Digest* would become.

It has been over four decades since Mario came into my professional and personal life. I remember when he took me to see Bobby Short perform in the Carlyle Hotel shortly after we met. I remember thinking, "This is work?"

The world knows him now. And, he is still part of my personal life. My friend Mario.

Paige Rense
Editor Emeritus
Architectural Digest

Favoring friends, chimpanzees, and dogs, my scrapboards are filled with personal photos and postcards I've been sent ... clockwise from upper left: Barbara Bancroft; Mario peering through a standing floral tribute of red gladioli he sent to Judy Green for his 60th birthday celebration she hosted with a card reading "Sorry we can't be with you, Barbara and Frank Sinatra;" Barbara Walters at the Wilbur Rosses' housewarming party; Dame Edna, whom Mario has seen perform ninety-eight times and counting, looking over California friends and baby Mario; Hilary and Wilbur Ross; bewigged with a client wearing a plastic baboushka with pink rollers; cousin Theresa in Aunt Mary's garden; receiving an honorary degree from Curtis High School presented by Richard E. Diamond, publisher of the Staten Island Advance; *with Slim Keith holding parasol; with Ann Rapp, Cathy Hardwick, and Joan Kron.*

IF YOU CAN'T HIDE IT, DECORATE IT

Reminiscences on a Life of Decoration

BY MARIO BUATTA

The all-white Buatta family living room

WHEN I WAS A LITTLE BOY, my mother said to me, "Piccolo Mario, what do you want to be when you grow up?" I shrugged, "I don't know—I don't want to play the violin like Poppa." "Maybe you should be an actor because you like to be on the stage." My brother said, "Well, maybe you should be a psychiatrist because you're so crazy." My father said, "Perhaps you should be a lawyer because you have such a big mouth." So I combined all three in order to become an interior decorator—an actor to convince my clients that I like their existing furniture, a psychiatrist to figure out what they like and don't like, and a lawyer to collect the bills!

From a young age, I was always aware of my surroundings. I grew up on Staten Island in Livingston Heights. It was like small-town America—

a great place to grow up. We lived in an English Tudor-style house—a door in the front and a door in the back—built by my grandfather. All the rooms were white and decorated in pure 1930s Deco. In the living room the furniture was placed around the walls as if my parents were about to give a dinner dance. The curtains—made for our previous Tudor City apartment, which had higher ceilings—puddled out two feet on the floor. You never knew whether it was raining, snowing, or sunny! The curtains were satiny, woven with wheat sheaves, and hung on steel poles with mirrored diamond-shaped finials. There was a chartreuse mohair-covered chesterfield with brown bullion-fringe trim and two satin pillows in chocolate brown with brush fringe, and a brown chenille tub chair with white piping. My mother always allowed

OPPOSITE *When I give a talk, I come out on stage—wearing a wig— and announce its title, "If You Can't Hide It, Decorate It." I drop the wig to the floor, which always makes the audience laugh. I then say I came from a family of dogs, who all had a lot more hair than I did.*

Buatta family photos, clockwise from top: Mario with his parents, Felix and Olive, in California, circa 1937; Mario's glamorous Aunt Mary, circa 1970; Felix and Olive with Mario's younger brother, Joseph, at his confirmation; Mario with his father; Mario with his mother and Aunt Mary in 1940; center: Mario, age three.

My mother always allowed me to rearrange the furniture—I'd stay up late thinking about where everything could go. Only the walnut parlor grand piano in the corner gave me a problem, as it was too heavy to move.

me to rearrange the furniture—I'd stay up late thinking about where everything could go. Only the walnut parlor grand piano in the corner gave me a problem, as it was too heavy to move.

I used to call our living room a "dead room" because we never used it. I'd ask my mother, "Why do we have this room?" And she'd reply, "For guests, for company." "But they never come here; we never see them!" She answered, "When you get your own house, you can do exactly what you want." My mother was like Joan Crawford in *Harriet Craig*. She would clean the ashtrays before anyone could finish a cigarette. She would vacuum herself out of the house so we could see if anybody had been there when we came home. You couldn't sit on the furniture or you'd make fanny prints, or touch the glass-top tables or you'd make fingerprints. She had an obsessive behavior. I always preferred the houses of my Waspy friends where it looked like they had lived in them, with books, magazines, and flowers everywhere.

My bedroom was a very pale blue with maple furniture, including a bookcase my grandfather made for me. There was a Mondrianesque carpet on the floor in browns and tans, and in the summertime it was changed out for plaid sisal. It was a very boring room. When I was sixteen, I was allowed to redecorate it. I wanted it to look like the inside of a barn, so I picked out a dark chocolate brown paint for the walls and a red for the inside of the closet. The doors were maple and had raised Deco paneling. The floor was wall-to-wall forest green carpeting. At the windows I had bamboo shades and plaid corduroy curtains that matched the bedspreads. There was a nonworking fireplace on one

wall, which my mother explained was for Santa to use at Christmas. I hung an old American gaslight, and over time with all the antiques I was collecting, it started to look like a shop.

My mother's entire family lived on the same hill. At the top lived her sister, Mary. I was always at her house, with its Chickendale, Hecklewhite, and Chinooserie antiques, light floral chintzes for the summer and black floral chintzes for the winter, and all sorts of wonderful things. I used to go shopping with her and her W. & J. Sloane decorator in Manhattan. We'd take the ferry and then a taxi to the uptown antiques shops. One day when she was shown a little needlepoint rug to go in front of the fireplace in the den, I said to her, "It's got worn spots—can't you afford a new rug?" The decorator almost hit me on the head!

Aunt Mary was like Auntie Mame, always trying out the latest style. We used to sit through Barbara

"Wherever I go, I have an urgent need to redecorate. Is that a sin, Father?"

One of the first things I bought was
an eighteenth-century lap desk from
a Third Avenue dealer for twelve dollars,
paying it off at fifty cents a week.
Years later, I showed my father a photo
of a similar desk offered at the
Winter Antiques Show for $4,500.

Stanwyck and Joan Crawford movies two or three times—because she'd be sketching the clothes that she'd then have made up by her seamstress. She followed trends, and the magazines were her bible. If she read that this season Mediterranean was in, she'd have to have a Mediterranean room. Her bedroom was French provincial with a John Widdicomb bedroom suite with a floral chintz canopy over the bed and a mirror-topped dressing table draped in the same fabric. In the dining room she brought in Molla metal garden furniture painted a pale, antiqued turquoise and put up scenic wallpaper of Southern plantation houses and gardens. The curtain pelmets were scalloped on top so it had the feeling of a Chinese pagoda roof. It was romantic and you felt like you were eating al fresco. She had the most beautiful gardens and was always winning prizes for them. She was very creative, but very competitive—she always had to make something different from and better than anyone else. I developed an eye for things and that was because of Aunt Mary.

By the age of eleven, I was collecting. One of the first things I bought was an eighteenth-century lap desk from a Third Avenue dealer for twelve dollars, paying it off at fifty cents a week. When I finally took it home, my father wouldn't let me bring it into the house. He said it was full of vermin and that I didn't know where it had been. He considered all antiques secondhand furniture. So I put the desk in the garage and sprayed it for three days—probably more things crawled into it than out! Finally he let me take it inside. I took it to my room and put it at the foot of my bed on top of a bench that I had made in shop class—the first and last thing I ever made. Years later, I showed my father a photo of a similar desk offered at the Winter Antiques Show for $4,500. My father said, "That's your desk!" When I told him it was another one, he exclaimed, "You were a fool! You should have bought more!"

When I was eighteen and could finally drive, I started going to the antiques shops on the island on my own. I remember a Battersea enamel box from the country dealer Virginia Sloane—every Sunday my friend Jean and I would race to her store. Jean wanted the box, so I let her buy it, and twenty years ago she gave it to me. I keep it next to my bed.

My mother and I used to drive around Staten Island and New Jersey just to gaze at houses. I enjoyed looking at architecture. My favorite building as a child was the Alice Austen House, originally a Dutch farmhouse that was made over into a Carpenter Gothic cottage in 1847. We'd go by and see it all the time. I loved the crisscross-paned windows and gingerbread decoration. Miss Austen was the first recognized American female photographer and the first woman to own a car on the island.

I spent a lot of time with my grandfather Joseph Destefani. My mother's father was a private housebuilder and as a hobby made very fine mandolins and guitars. His brother designed chandeliers and had volumes of his own designs. He was born in Sicily in 1875 and married my grandmother Rose, who was born in New York. Their house, which he designed and built, was a typical center-hall colonial. It had white peach trees in the garden and a second kitchen in the basement where he made wine. He

BUATTA FAMILY TREE

PATERNAL GRANDFATHER MARINO BUATTA *arrived in New York in 1870 to mail a letter because the postal service in Italy was so slow.*

MATERNAL GRANDFATHER JOSEPH DESTEFANI *came to the States to fight in the Civil War.*

PAPÀ FELIX *who-sa make-a da pasta.*

AUNT LENA AND UNCLE SANCTIS *are pictured with their divorce decree.*

MAMMA OLIVE *stopped by on her way to the beauty parlor and sat on my Louis XVI chair; she said it was very uncomfortable.*

MARIO AND BROTHER, GIUSEPPE, *pose in the glorious Staten Island countryside.*

COUSINS THERESA AND DOROTHY, *long-haired brats.*

The Buatta Family crest has a tree with dogs running around the trunk, chasing one another.

My favorite house to visit as a child was the Alice Austen House on Staten Island.

was an amazing man who did everything—he reminded me of Burt Lancaster in *The Leopard*.

My Uncle Saviore was an architect and used to design houses with and for my grandfather to build. He died when I was five, and my grandfather thought I would be the next architect in the family. "Look at the houses," he would always say. All my textbooks were filled with drawings of houses. After high school, I went to Cooper Union, where Saviore had graduated, but I hated it. Nine weeks later my mother died and I had to leave—I took off and never went back. I went in for decorating—I didn't want to learn mathematics. I wasn't interested in how a house was constructed; I wanted to know about elements like moldings, columns, and shapes of rooms.

My father's father, for whom I was named, was from a long line of renowned stuccodores and left Sicily in 1870 after a disagreement with his father. I first saw Sicily in about 1970. I met my cousins in Palermo and Catania; they spoke only Italian and French, so I didn't understand what they were saying,

Some came by boat. My family came by land, and we brought David with us. I like to joke that I come from a long line of Italian-Indians—the Sioux-Sicilians. An ancestor, Guido, was an artist who worked on the Sistine Chapel. He didn't like heights, so he painted the baseboards. I also had a cousin who was at The Last Supper. He was seated at table 43.

but they were very nice people. In later years I was fortunate to meet the Baronessa Antonella Canalotti. Together we toured many palazzos and villas where I noticed fancy plasterwork. I would pull out a notepad and say to our host, "Oh yes, the Graziano family . . . I see here that you didn't pay the entire bill." Everyone would laugh.

I have always been proud of my Italian heritage. We had a neighbor who always walked around with her nose in the air. When I was eight or nine, I asked my mother what was her attitude all about. She replied, "Her forebears came over on the *Mayflower*." A few years later they were moving and outside of the house were these big vans labeled Mayflower Moving and Storage. I told my mother, "Look! Mrs. Adams is going back on the *Mayflower*."

My father, Felix, played violin from the age of eight, and at thirteen he was playing at the Marconi Hotel and Restaurant on Staten Island. My dad had a wonderful career. He played with Rudy Vallee and the Connecticut Yankees for over twelve years. In the late thirties, we lived in California while Vallee was making movies. Alice Faye, the actress and singer, was my babysitter. Years later, in the 1970s, I ran into her at P.J. Clarke's, where she pretended she would have been far too young to have looked after me. After Vallee disbanded the Yankees in 1940, we moved back east to Staten Island. My father became a society bandleader at the Savoy Plaza Hotel under the stage name Phil Burton and accompanied many entertainers on Broadway, including Edith Piaf when she played at the supper club Versailles.

When I was thirteen, my father retired from the business and opened up Buatta's Music Center, a piano showroom and music store in Stapleton. I went into Manhattan three days a week to buy records, and also styled the shop. He would get angry because this was always here, but then the week after it was there, and then over there. He said, "I can't find anything!" I said, "But, Dad, if you leave it in one place all the time, it won't look like you have anything new. You have to merchandise your goods." In 1952 a record came out called *It's in the Book*. I put big letters I had cut out in the window that said "It's in the Book" and we must have sold one hundred copies in a week. I didn't believe in collecting records at that

Felix Buatta playing first violin with Rudy Vallee, standing, and the Connecticut Yankees.

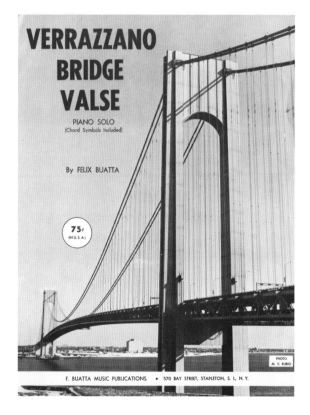

"Verrazzano Bridge Valse"—the sheet music is now a collector's item—was written by Felix Buatta in 1964 in honor of the opening of the bridge connecting Staten Island to Brooklyn.

19

A bedroom I did for the August 1975 issue of House & Garden, *inspired by Albert Hadley's summer bedroom that had been featured in* Vogue.

time—I thought it was a waste of money. Eventually I became very serious about collecting recordings— Peggy Lee, Frank Sinatra, and Broadway shows like *The Boyfriend* with Julie Andrews. In later years I was lucky enough to get personally acquainted with Peggy Lee, Blossom Dearie, and others—their music was in my blood. When I first met Miss Lee, in 1984, I was instantly intoxicated. I even flew out to Los Angeles to see her perform ten nights in a row. Whenever she performed in New York, I never missed a show.

I thought I wanted to be an actor. When I was in my first year of college, I took a speech class. The professor, who ran a theater group at a local museum, said, "You don't need to take this course—you're wasting your credits. You should take something else. Would you like to join our group?" They put me in the play *Oh Men! Oh Women!* as a steward on a ship. I had to bring the bags in for a certain lady and said, "Madame, where would you like me to put your bags?" "Cut!" he exclaimed, "It's not Madame, it's not French—it's Madam." So I'd go on again and say, "Where would you like me to put your bags, Madame?" Cut! He went crazy with me. That was the first play I was in. One summer, I was cast as a reporter in a play called *Solid Gold Cadillac* at the local country club. All I had to say was "UPI," but I would say "UPS." So the next play I was pulling the curtain, and then the next one I was selling ads for the program.

During college I worked at Bonwit Teller as head of stock of the gift shop run by Pauline Van der Voort Rogers, who was married to Walter Hoving, the head of Tiffany & Co. It was very special and had wonderful things—porcelain, crystal, silver—all top quality. She would go to France to find things and was very particular. It was a great learning experience.

In 1959 I got a job at B. Altman & Co. Within two months I took an opening in the decorating department as an assistant. Home furnishings took up the entire seventh floor. The decorating department was on the floor above, next to the very popular Charleston Gardens restaurant, whose interior featured a real plantation facade. At that time they had thirty decorators and they had just finished redoing several rooms of the White House. People always said you'd have Sloane's do your first

floor and B. Altman's do your second floor. They had a lot of prestigious clients and they had good decorators. At night I took drafting courses at Pratt and courses in the decorative arts at Columbia.

I took a room at 55 West 11th Street in Greenwich Village. It was the servant's room in the artist Kenzo Okada's house, with two windows overlooking the garden. I was there for about a year, until a friend invited me to share a three-bedroom apartment on 10th Street, which was good, as I needed more space for my collections.

One day Albert Hadley, then at McMillen, walked into the antiques department at Altman's. I knew who he was from a summer bedroom he did in *Vogue* in 1959 for $200, a room that I loved and had torn out of the magazine. He introduced himself and recommended that I study in Europe with Stanley Barrows, who ran the Parsons European summer session. Stanley was wonderful—very droll. He was like a favorite uncle. He wore a fedora and blue blazer, and had a monotone voice. He was funny and the students all loved him. He knew how to keep us awake by telling us all the wicked things, like *that* was the door the mistress would come in through.

Cline On Design RICHARD CLINE

"This is John. The Mario Buatta of Westport."

21

I first saw Villa Foscari (La Malcontenta) when I traveled to nearby Vicenza with the Parsons School of Design summer program in 1961. I was impressed by the octagonal center table, banquettes, and trompe-l'oeil decoration.

Sometime in the 1980s I spent an entire weekend at Drottningholm, location of the royal residence of Sweden. I love the interiors of the Chinese Pavilion— reminiscent of the later Brighton Pavilion.

On Saturdays I worked for the eccentric Rose Cumming, along with Tom Britt, John Robert Moore II, and a few others, in her house on 53rd Street to save up for the Parsons course. She paid us each ten dollars for the day to dust lightly and move things to her shop on Park Avenue, formerly an automobile showroom that she had painted a deep purple. At the end of the day she prepared dinner for the four or so of us. We sat at the mirror-topped dining table on eighteenth-century red lacquered chairs under a cloudy cerulean blue ceiling. The floors were black and the walls were mirrored with mercury glass. She prepared sautéed canned tuna and cherry tomatoes together with frozen peas whose green dye swirled around the plate. One particular night she appeared at the entrance to the dining room with a large silver tray filled with the above. Looking radiant with purple hair, strands of green jade beads around her neck, and a rather lowish décolletage—glamorously lit by several dozen black candles—she suddenly tripped on the saddle of the door opening. Without a second to spare, she scooped the dinner back onto the tray and exclaimed how lucky it was we had cleaned that day!

Later on I shopped at her store for fabrics. She had the most wonderful chintzes. One time I borrowed a half-dozen fabric samples for a house in Tulsa that I was doing. While traveling, I suffered a burst appendix and was hospitalized. Two months later, after having lost thirty pounds, I went back to her shop to return the samples and place an order. She said I looked weak and sat me down at her desk. She opened a lower drawer and took out a teapot and two cups into which she proceeded to pour healthy portions. Passersby looked in and thought how civilized we were with a cup of tea in each of our hands. When I took it to my lips, I discovered it was brandy and, as I was not a drinker, said, "Er, em ..." She replied, "It will be good for you!"

In 1961 I did the Parsons program from May until late September and stayed overseas until the end of the year. There were about twenty of us, including Ronald Bricke, Mary Louise Guertler, and Hope Brown. We took the *Liberté* to Southampton and did a tour of country houses, followed by a few weeks in London. It's funny, because at that time I

Charles de Beistegui's dining room at the Château de Groussay in France is another room I admire. He was also influenced by La Malcontenta.

was not impressed with the dry and dull decorating of the English country houses I saw.

In Paris we visited the Musée d'Art Moderne. After we looked at Matisses and Bonnards, Professor Barrows turned to the class and said, "These are the most brilliant colorists, and if you don't understand what these painters are doing, you'll never be a good decorator." I've always remembered that. After the course was over in September, I went to Greece, Germany, Spain, and Portugal, where I had olive sandwiches for lunch and could live on five dollars a day.

McMillen, Inc. decorated this bedroom for Gregory Smith. The brown lacquered Regency bed from the Brighton Pavilion is said to have been made for Prince Albert. I acquired the bed for myself in the 1970s, when Mr. Smith moved.

In the 1970s, Parsons stopped teaching historical design—they would teach only the twentieth century. Stanley left for FIT in 1971. If you don't know about the eighteenth and nineteenth centuries, you can't decorate for the twenty-first. There's no way. You have to understand history and how furnishings were laid out in rooms. The best arrangements of furniture in the eighteenth century were always punctuated by a settee and several chairs set around it in a crescent. You can use that principle by creating a circular arrangement with two chairs flanking a sofa, and either two more looking in or an ottoman. Understanding and appreciating this begins in the schools.

When I returned from Europe, I went out to interview. My first choice, like everybody else's, was Billy Baldwin, who said he would keep me in mind. I would have liked to have interviewed with Mrs. Henry Parish II, but I knew she had only one assistant, and it was my best friend, Richard Nelson, so I couldn't go there. Her rooms were cozy and comfortable, but conservative. She always used the same repertoire of window valances and the same colors of apricot, pale yellow, and pale green. She did have the gift of making houses and rooms look very lived-in. When Albert Hadley joined the firm in 1962, they became the greatest team since Nancy Lancaster and John Fowler. Everything they did was just magic. Sister, as Mrs. Parish was known to her friends, made her rooms look very inviting, and you felt like people had just left the room.

Sister also had an amusing touch. Look at the cottages in Maine that she had—they were all very whimsical. They became more so when Albert came along, because his more modernist approach pushed her out of her comfort zone. Sister took Albert's architectural rooms and made them into something livable and wonderful. If you look at the rooms Sister did many years ago, they still have that look of having always been there and not recently decorated. Like me, she called her style the undecorated look, and that's what it was, with elements from every period, every country, humble and formal, all jumbled together. It doesn't come across as though it was all shopped for yesterday— it looks as though it's been there forever. It has a sense of belonging and a sense of timelessness.

I did this setting, which was part of a tribute to Billy Baldwin and his clients, with Baldwin slipper chairs covered in a coral and trellis print from my first collection of fabrics. I dedicated the space to Jacqueline Onassis. I first met her at a birthday party for her sister, Lee Radziwill, where I unknowingly tore the seat of my trousers when I sat down. After the incident, she came up to me and was very kind.

Sister Parish was one of my icons. After she saw a show-house space, a landing,
I did with Lee Jofa Floral Bouquet chintz and aubergine walls, she exclaimed,
"I'm using that in my drawing room!" I teased her, "You copycat!"

I also met with McMillen, who told me I didn't have any schooling. Someone then recommended Elisabeth Draper, who was married to Dorothy Draper's ex-husband. Her firm was located in an enfilade of rooms on the second floor of the Rhinelander house on the corner of Madison and 72nd Street, where Ralph Lauren is today. Mrs. Draper was at the end room facing all of us like a headmistress. My desk was where the men's dressing room is now. She had a very big name and had important clients like the Eisenhowers, the Houghtons, and the Auchinclosses.

It has been said that behind every great woman decorator is a man, and the combination is necessary because you need the man for the architecture and proportion, and the woman to soften it and furnish it and make it look like your home. Mrs. Draper's was a fellow called Jack Braden who used to do all the Baker furniture showrooms and had a lot of style. It was a great beginning for me.

That same year I bought the British edition of *The House & Garden Book of Interiors*, which featured many rooms by John Fowler. I didn't know who John Fowler was, but when I looked at his rooms, they spoke to me. I opened up a double-page spread and there was Nancy Lancaster's "buttah yeller" room. I had never seen anything like it when I was a student, and it just knocked my eyes out. The color was wonderful, but it was also that everything in the room was an amalgamation of all the things that she had collected from all the great houses she lived in over the decades—everything in it was so personal.

While working for Mrs. Draper, George Schreyer, whom I met at Altman's, called and said, "I'm associated with a firm looking for an assistant. His name is Keith Irvine and he used to work for John Fowler and for Mrs. Henry Parish, and you would fit right in." I walked into Keith's office and was totally taken in. There were different shades of yellow and white moldings on the wall, a pale blue ceiling, and a chintz sofa—a small chesterfield covered in Lee Jofa's Floral Bouquet chintz. Everything else was mix and match and it was just beautiful.

Keith lived and worked on the second floor of a brick house in the East 70s. There was a big square room with a long hallway leading to the offices. I would often go out with Keith and his friend Chippy (later his wife) to cabarets and clubs. I would spend my whole salary—we had a lot of fun. They liked to think they were Fred Astaire and Ginger Rogers, dancing up and down staircases. I invited them home to meet my Aunt Mary—Keith was undone by her.

I worked for Keith for a year. I learned more about English style. Everyone else was doing the French taste that was very popular in the 1950s—stiff, staid, and proper. Keith had a lot of flair and was very theatrical. His work was more Victorian compared to John Fowler's, which was more true to the eighteenth and early nineteenth centuries.

In May of '63, I started my own firm and moved into an apartment at 1007 Lexington Avenue, four flights up and eighty-five dollars a month. It was an L-shaped room I had painted eggplant and in which I used the same Floral Bouquet chintz that I've been using since the beginning. Sister later copied that combination in her own living room after seeing a landing I did in the late 1970s for a Kips Bay show house. For over fifty years I have lived with this chintz in six different apartments and I have never gotten tired of it—I even had trousers made out of it! The colors are great. There was also a little kitchen and a bathroom I did in El Morocco blue and white zebra fabric. In 1999 I returned to 1007 Lexington to decorate the restaurant Swifty's, on the ground floor, with Anne Eisenhower.

Around this time in the early sixties, one of my first clients gave me a copy of a book on Beauport, the summer house of Henry Davis Sleeper in Gloucester, Massachusetts. I was instantly mesmerized and went to visit it with Professor Barrows. As houses were being torn down and sold in the early twentieth century, Sleeper and his mother would purchase complete rooms and add them on to the house. Each of the forty rooms is a small version of a big room and is dedicated to a different theme or period. It's essentially a collection of collections. I loved the Octagon Room, which has red toleware arranged against eggplant walls—I never forgot that color combination. Sleeper was one of America's first professional decorators, and he advised Henry du Pont on Winterthur in Wilmington, Delaware.

The eggplant color of this room at Beauport—Henry Davis Sleeper's house in Gloucester, Massachusetts—is what I chose to paint my first apartment.

My clients Sandra and Nelson Doubleday were hesitant to invite me to their Christmas party in the country because, without my assistance, they had used Floral Bouquet chintz, which they mistakenly thought was my design. As a joke, I had a pair of trousers made up in the fabric to wear when I visited them, and they took this photograph, which they presented to me in a frame at their New Year's Day lunch. On my tassel loafers I tied tartan bows that were used as napkin rings at a dinner party the night before. The hostess saw me and demanded them back!

*John Fowler sitting in his new Garden Room
at the Hunting Lodge, his country house.*

I returned to London in 1964 and walked around, retracing my steps from when I was there as a student. I came across a shop whose window captured my attention. I looked up and saw it was Sybil Colefax and John Fowler's showroom. I went to the front door, but it was closed for the lunch hour. I knocked and the caretaker came out. When I told him that I had worked for Mr. Irvine, he asked me if I'd like to meet Mr. Fowler. He got him on the phone and instructed me to come back at 6 p.m. When I returned, John was sitting at his desk wearing the same pocket square that I had bought earlier in the day—blue with red and white etching like penwork. He was laughing. I took out my overly filled index cards listing whom and what I wanted to see: "I'd like to meet Cecil Hicks, David Beaton, and Elsa Lanchester," and he started laughing again. "Dear boy, you have it all wrong—it's David Hicks, Cecil Beaton, and Nancy Lancaster!" We talked and laughed.

John was a scholar—he knew color, he knew period, he knew everything. His office was a rather large room, and one whole wall was all samples of silks that had been dyed. He had pink, red, red-pink, blue-pink, orange-pink, yellow-pink, green-pink—it was just amazing. He'd take snips and he'd scheme the jobs that way. Everything was dyed specially—nothing was plain or used as is.

The next evening he took me to Mrs. Lancaster's house next door, which had the big yellow room that I wanted to see. She received us in her bedroom since she had the vapors. She said, "Oh, dreadful Americans! I had forty sets of dirty sheets at Haseley [her country house] last month." I thought she must be someone else, as I knew Nancy Lancaster was American. I turned to Mr. Fowler and asked, "What did you say the lady's name was again?" The phone rang and he eared me into the hallway. He said to the secretary, "This man is so rude. He just insulted Mrs. Lancaster." The next day I made sure to send her some of her favorite chocolate truffles.

John invited me to come stay for the weekend at the Hunting Lodge, his country house, and said we could stop by Haseley Court on the way for tea. When we drove up, Nancy came running out of the house and said, "How dare you bring this dreadful man!" I was still sitting in the car and I thought, holy moly, I'm not turning off the motor. She was hugging him and winking at me, and then he barked, "Get out of the car, you damn fool!" She then showed us the house. She'd say, "He doesn't want to see this." But John answered, "Yes, he does! He's interested." So she opened every door so I could see every nook and cranny. What was really great were the entrance hall with the odd bits of blue and white Delft, and a wing chair covered in Delft-patterned needlepoint.

Years later when I was a weekend guest at Haseley, Nancy had an ancient personal maid who could have been in her nineties at the time. She gave Mrs. Lancaster her white gloves, which were really more gray than white. "I washed them three times—if you think you can do better, why don't you give it a try?" One day the maid passed out on the floor and Mrs. Lancaster brought the spirits of ammonia. She said, "Where am I, where am I?" Nancy replied, "You're in hell, dear, and I am *your* lady's maid."

Nancy Lancaster's "buttah yeller" drawing room is my favorite room. It speaks of the past, the present, the future. It's a scrapbook of her life.

When we left Haseley, the car I had rented for the week ran out of gas about a mile from the house, and John was hysterical. I had to thumb a ride to get gas and bring it back. At the end of my visit, I was standing in the little sitting room admiring two of John's paintings of auricula by Samuel Dixon. He came in and said, "Bloody fool, what are you doing now?" "I'm just looking at these pictures." "Come along, you'll see them again—you'll see them again!"

I would return three times a year—I used to take those twenty-one-day excursions so I'd be there over three weekends, and John would always invite me out. We would visit friends and clients of his—there would always be some Lady Umpty Ump or a former showgirl who was a humpback. There would also be one of the decorators from the shop, and the lampshade lady would be there as well. We'd go to see these people and they'd ask, "How are you enjoying your visit?" And I'd say, "It's terrible, my bed has a huge sinking hole in the middle; it's like sleeping in a hammock." John would be mortified but they'd laugh. I once wrapped up a tulip vase of his and gave it to him as a present. He was absolutely delighted and said to his assistant, "Oh, Billy, go downstairs and look in the cupboard—I might have one exactly the same. Wouldn't that be marvelous?" And of course he would find that it was missing from the cupboard and laugh.

His friend Lady Bonham Carter was always there. She was eighty-eight-years-old and she drove a car. You'd hear the car pull up and it would take her ten minutes before she entered, as she was changing into her fancy dress in the car. After dinner we'd take coffee in the sitting room and she'd nod off. I once put a whoopee cushion in the club chair next to the fireplace where John always sat, but she sat there that evening and it went off. She said, "Ooh, I'm so sorry."

I used to send John a letter every few weeks about everything that was happening in New York. It was typewritten and I would sign it "Billy [Baldwin], Betsey [Whitney], Bunny [Mellon], and Sister send their best." I barely knew any of these people, but he thought I knew them. While visiting John over the Christmas holiday, I had already had it up to here with being in the country by Boxing Day.

Sister was also in London to do the Charles and Jane Engelhard apartment and wanted to come out to see John's new garden room. While I was getting dressed to go into the city to see a film, I overheard John say on the telephone, "Oh, Sister, I have no one here. I can't give you a meal but I can give you tea. There are some wonderful lemon clusters." I decided I better stick around as I had secretly eaten them all and had to make a fresh batch without John knowing. When Sister arrived, she gave me away by remarking on the wonderful baking aroma. We later went in to watch television because someone was landing on the moon. I turned to her and asked how was the weather in New York and if there was still a lot of snow. She replied, "Oh, have you been visiting New York?" And John exclaimed, "He told me he was your best friend. I knew he was a phony!" She was taken aback by the whole thing, but he got a kick out of it and had a ball making fun of me.

When Sister got back to New York, she told John Robert Moore II, one of her talented assistants, "I met this Mario Butero and he made a fool out of me. I had no idea he had told John he knew me." I used to play a lot of tricks on her. There was a dealer who used to work at Colefax and Fowler as an antiques buyer. She was quite a character with an over-powdered nose and an Hermès scarf always around her head. When she opened up her own shop, she asked me to call on her. I was over with clients to shop the Grosvenor House show and wasn't able to stop by. She said, "You haven't been to see me and I have all these lovely new things and Mrs. Parish is coming to see me next week." I told her I would come by in the early morning and look in the window. I took a yellow sheet of paper and jotted down everything I liked, and wrote: "Please send them as soon as possible, Mrs. Parish." She called the Parish Hadley office, and Albert rang me up and asked if this was one of my practical jokes. I answered, "I'm afraid so." I then ran into Sister a few days later at one of the workrooms. She came in and said, "Oh, it's you. Well, one of your jokes just backfired in a big way"—as the dealer was upset. Mrs. Parish had a wicked sense of humor—you could tease her. She used to joke that I'd call and ask her, "What have you done lately that I can copy?" She

"I wish we had tiptoed, not jumped, into wicker."

respected what I did and admired my decorating. In later years she invited me for a drink and asked me, "What is it you're doing? Decorating; public speaking; designing lamps, potpourri, bed linens, furniture—what is it you're going to be?" I said to her, "All of the above." She was speechless.

In 1966 I moved to an apartment on 72nd Street between Park and Lexington. Inspired by Rose Cumming, I covered the walls with silver tea paper, and painted the woodwork green and the floors black. As always, there was the same Lee Jofa chintz at the windows. The kitchen was done in black semi-gloss paint with white appliances and a black and white floor. Albert visited and he loved this little tub chair that I had slipcovered very baggy so that it looked like the ones you'd see in an English country house. He asked if he could move it, and he shifted it two inches. It made all the difference. That's when you pick up lessons in your life. He noticed the paper in my bathroom, which was a Philip Graf black and white chain-link design, and declared, "You copied that from my bathroom!" I said, "I know." He then asked if he could copy the silver paper, so I gave him the source and he used it in his own apartment.

I wasn't published in a national magazine until 1969. It was a bright yellow bedroom with a coral-colored canopy bed with floral chintz hangings for a Greenwich show house. *House & Garden* said they weren't going to take a picture of the room, but then they decided to put it in the magazine and asked me if I wanted to come to their offices and see the layout. That's when I met Diana Vreeland in the elevator. I imagine she was shocked when I jumped in the elevator with her, because they probably always sent her up right away and by herself. She asked, "Who are you?" And I replied, "Nobody special." She returned, "I'm sure that's not true." She was very nice. That photo really was the turning point. Mrs. Samuel I. Newhouse saw it, called Mary Jane Pool, the editor of *House & Garden*, to find out who did it, and hired me to copy the room for her country house in New Jersey.

I showed John Fowler a photo of my next apartment, which was published in the January 1970 issue of *House & Garden*. It had a yellow living room with decorative taffeta sash hung pictures and brackets everywhere supporting blue and white Delft jars. He said, "Young man, if you're going to copy me, you could've done a better job." I said, "Mr. Fowler, I didn't copy you. I was *inspired* by you." He once gave me a color, a yellow, but I didn't use it. I made it brighter since colors in England aren't clear and don't look the same over here because the light is different. In America, brighter colors look better.

I have a painterly way of decorating. Composing a room is like taking a canvas and putting color on a little bit at a time. Most clients don't understand this and want to see a rendering of exactly how it's going to look when you're finished. They also don't understand that you have to have varying sizes of things in a room; everything can't be at the same level or it will look like a sea. It should be like a garden where things are growing at all different heights. I always say that I'm bringing the outdoors in and that a room grows like a garden over the years. You continue to add to it, you subtract from it, you add things you've been left, add things you've found, better things than you had there before. No room is ever finished—it's continually evolving and changes as you change.

Many English country houses have been lived in by several generations, and each one has left their personal collections of whimsy and eccentricity behind. It's all there for the eighth or ninth generation to enjoy and talk about. It says so much about the family's history. On the other side of the coin, the average American moves seven or eight

"Think this is bad? You should see the inside of my head."

times in their lifetime, leaving much behind and starting afresh in the latest decorating style. It's like not having any old friends around, only new ones.

A show-house room is different—it's showbiz and has to be a statement. The blue and white bedroom I did for the Kips Bay Show House in 1984 has become one of my most famous rooms over the years (see pages 222–223). George Oakes, Colefax and Fowler's design director, hadn't even stepped into the entire room before he exclaimed, "There's everything but the kitchen sink in here! You have one of everything going on in this room." A client fell in love with this fantasy room and asked me to give her the same bed hung with white linen curtains from the ceiling. When her husband walked in and saw it, he demanded, "Do real men sleep in beds like this?" I answered *yes* nervously and left. I called the house the next day and the next, with no reply. The maid said they hadn't left their room. Monday morning I heard this little voice on the phone, "Are you trying to kill me?" "What, did the canopy fall on you?" "No, my husband fell into bed Friday night and never got out. It was the most romantic thing that's ever happened to me."

At the beginning of any project, I first look at the architecture. It should be the best it can be, and if it can be changed, the time to do it is at the beginning. I then think about how the clients are going to use the rooms. I have often stayed with them

over a weekend to see firsthand how they use the rooms. Will they be there only at night during the week and then in the country on weekends? If so, they might choose to decorate with darker and more intense colors and with low pools of light so that the house looks best at night, because that's when they're there. Then I do the color plan to decide which colors are suitable and how they flow from one room to another.

I then start thinking about the furniture plan. As soon as I enter a room, I immediately see how the furniture should be arranged—it's the sort of thing that becomes second nature with experience. The client is always perplexed and asks, "How did you think of that?" I say, "It's all I think about." Sometimes the client will request we try out other layouts, but we almost always end up right back with the first one. When I go to people's houses, whether I'm a guest or I'm there because they hired me, I'm rearranging their furniture all the time in my head.

Arrange your furniture in groupings—think of it as if the pieces were, in a sense, talking to each other. One of the best ways to figure out how your room works best is to have a party. The next morning, you will see how your guests moved all your furniture around the room to make conversing easier. I try to create this arrangement before the guests arrive. It's very important to have furniture not placed randomly—a chair over here, a sofa here, a lamp over there, a table over there. There is nothing more awkward than arriving at a party and having to scurry about finding a chair to join a group of friends. Select the upholstered pieces first, like the sofa, to make sure your room sits well. You should buy the best custom-made upholstery you can find, because you will have it for the rest of your life, and the older it gets, the more comfortable it feels and looks.

The finishing touches are as important as anything. One client wanted to cut down on a curtain's trimmings. Well, it's the trimmings that make the curtain. She didn't understand the connection between that and, for example, a genuine Chanel suit. Without those wonderful buttons or those two colors on the edges, what would you have? A plain white suit with plain buttons. Fill your rooms with objects and furnishings that reflect your feelings

"Our dream is to live long enough to see the end of our renovation."

HOUSE & GARDEN'S
BEST IN
DECORATION

and dreams. Think about having summer schemes and winter themes—like changing your tablescapes with the seasons. In the summer, in addition to slipcovers, my mother changed the carpet in every room of the house—the wool carpets were rolled up and stored, and sisal was put down.

The interior decorator's role is to create the stage setting for clients to act out their lives. If you placed Blanche DuBois from *A Streetcar Named Desire* in the set for Noël Coward's *Design for Living*, she wouldn't have known what to do. Decoration is a process that should grow with you, that changes as you change. You travel; you collect things; you inherit things, and people give you things. Our rooms become living backgrounds, a reflection of where we've been and where we are. The more personal the better, and even when you are not in the room, your presence should be felt.

My style isn't for everyone, and that's fine. Normally when prospective husband-and-wife clients come in, I sit them on the sofa and let them look at a portfolio of my work while I excuse myself. My secretary goes in and offers them a drink, which they always decline after looking around at all the dust—because everything *is* dusty. Unlike my mother, I think of dust as a protective coating for fine furniture. The clients think if it's this dusty here, what must the kitchen be like? And they are absolutely right. Meanwhile, I tiptoe back behind the screen to hear what they're saying. Sometimes the husband will remark, "Everything here is from the past; it looks like it was from my grandmother's house—let's go." But the wife says, "No, no, let's wait." I then come out and ask if everything's okay. The husband begs off and the missus says, "He just loves your apartment as it reminds him of his grandmother's house. Can you reproduce it for us?" I tell the wife, "Sure, but it doesn't happen overnight—it takes at least three years to get this much dust!"

My apartment today is full of things I've collected over the years. Clients and friends have asked if these are all family possessions? I answer, "Yes! But not my family." Everything here tells a story; it's a scrapbook of my life. Some of it is good, some of it is chipped or broken, but it's a collection. It's what John Fowler called "pleasing decay," which many don't understand today—if anything is worn out, they want to paint it right away or recover it. It means that something looks well-worn and lived with, and like an old pair of shoes that you love or an old jacket that gets better with age, it has character.

I don't buy for investment. I always tell clients, "Buy something because you like it or you need it." To me, an investment is stocks, bonds, or real estate. I'd rather look at a pair of candlesticks, a mirror, or a painting that gives me pleasure. That's the return I get. Everything I have may be old, but I love it all. It's the prose and poetry in my life.

Of course, for instant English-country-house style, you can take the recommendation I gave my client Taki Theodoracopulos, who once joshed that he had a townhouse in London that looked like a bordello in Miami Beach and a new house in New York, decorated by yours truly, that looked like it was in Eaton Square. I advised him in my quasi-Italian: "We glaze-a the walls nice colors, we put-a nice carpet and nice-a floral chintzes, nice-a paneled library, and for your wife, a four-a poster bed. Then-a on-a weekend before you-a move-a in, we put-a nice-a flowers, bowls-a water and bowls-a Alpo. We call-a ASPCA and borrow-a twenty-five dogs, lock up-a the house and Monday-a morning send-a the dogs-a back, clean-a up the house, and she look and a-smell like a Englishy country house, I'm-a promise-a you!"

Mario Buatta

Mario Buatta
a.k.a. The Prince of Chintz
New York City

37

Christopher Mason performing at a New York fete.

"The Prince of Chintz Song"
(excerpt)

To "The Stately Homes of England"

The English Country Style look
Was frankly dull and bleak
'Til this guy from Staten Island
Came along and made it chic!
His ruffles, bows and potpourris
Inspired thriving industries
As millions watched, entranced,
Tried to copy him,
But even landed dukes
Can't match his grand deluxe.

His famous doggy pictures
With ribbons on their frames
Became the rage on Park and Fifth
And even in St. James;
Four-poster beds were torn to shreds
To match Buatta's style:
The Cotswolds by way of Staten Island!

*"The Prince of Chintz Song" was written and performed by Christopher Mason
to celebrate the establishment of The Mario Buatta Atelier
at The New York School of Interior Design. The event took place at
the Metropolitan Club in New York on March 9, 2011.*

OPPOSITE *Mario sitting in a client's red lacquered library, circa 1976.*

ROOMS ARE
NEVER FINISHE

More from the world of Buatta ... from left: with colleague Tom Britt at Tom's 40th birthday celebration—
Mario donned a doctor's coat and stethoscope while he put Tom in a straightjacket that read: "40 and still on the loose;"
Marilyn White; Architectural Digest *editor-in-chief Margaret Russell; Alice Mason; Nan Kempner; Arlene Dahl; Herb Ritts*
man with tumbleweed hairdo; "The two-headed man reminds me of people who can't make up their minds," says Mario.
A Buattatude: A client's mother said to her daughter, "Why would you paint a room white when you could have color for the same price?"

BORN TO SHOP!

I'M NUTS ABOUT MUTTS
By MORT DIXON & HARRY WOODS

TOWN

Neoclassical House

Houston, Texas

The owners of this beautifully proportioned 1930s John Staub house were so enamored by the existing decoration done by Mario for the previous residents that they immediately hired him to revamp the interiors for their needs. The living room, with its gracious 11-foot-high ceiling, was glazed in daffodil yellow complemented by yellow plaid silk curtains. The result is a room that glows day and night. It also serves as a painterly backdrop for the clients' collection of important Impressionist paintings, although the decorator asserts, "I never think about paintings when designing a room, because eventually you might collect something else and switch it." The house's neoclassical style is played up with faux-marble painted walls in the entrance hall (below). A Colefax and Fowler star carpet is on the stairs.

42

LEFT and BELOW *Large windows at both ends of the living room flood the space with sunlight. Floral roundels on the Aubusson-style carpet and the Colefax and Fowler chintz bring a feeling of the garden indoors. A Chinese papered screen masks a doorway and grounds the room's frothy palette with its deep patination.*

The library's warm and comfortable interior makes it one of the most used rooms in the house. The clients wanted to keep the original stained paneling but they didn't want it too dark. Vibrant and colorful textiles, including Brunschwig & Fils chinoiserie chintz Le Lac, keep the scheme lively.

RIGHT *What once used to be a porch, open on three sides, is now an all-year sunroom overlooking the gardens. Mario designed the corner banquette with serpentine back. Wicker furniture, palm tree lamps, and a soft green and white herringbone chenille carpet retain the porchlike feel, but with all the comforts of being indoors.*

BELOW *In the dining room, the property's spectacular gardens inspired the shrimp pink walls, a floral trellis carpet, and green upholstery on the chairs. Over the mantel* Lady with a Parasol *by Frederick Carl Frieseke splendidly continues the* en plein air *mood.*

FOLLOWING SPREAD *The master bedroom is a blush color*
with an even paler pink-ground Lee Jofa chintz used
for the four-poster bed. On the slipper chair is a pale turquoise
lily block print from Jean Monro. Mario remarks,
"I love the idea of mixing several patterns. It's like a garden
with different flowers and plants—suddenly you see
a lot of this and then a lot of that. It grows over time."

ABOVE *Blue and white prints and porcelains make a crisp pairing with the apricot walls.*

LEFT *The 3,000-square-foot pool house pavilion was newly built by architects Curtis & Windham. Its scheme had to strike the perfect balance between formality and informality, as the clients entertained extensively here. The black and white floor was inspired by Claridge's lobby, the clients' preferred London hotel, with a broad Greek-key border riffing on Robert Adam's design for the entrance hall at Syon House. A mirror-top center table is encircled by four Chippendale-style chairs with silver-leaf legs and four towering palm trees fabricated from natural materials to dramatically soar up to the 19½-foot ceiling.*

53

Hilary and Wilbur Ross
Former Pied-à-Terre New York, New York

This thirtieth-floor Fifth Avenue penthouse boasted spectacular views as well as an equally superb art collection. A further consideration was the Rosses' legendary entertaining. Since the living room is used mostly in the evening, Mario chose a glamorous glossy eggplant, treated to look like porphyry, for the walls. "This is one of my favorite colors. It's what I used in my first apartment—a great color on which to display paintings, and at night it reflects the city lights." To achieve the effect, a base coat of bubblegum pink was put on. Mrs. Ross laughingly remembers her husband's alarm when he first saw it and thought it was the final color. A pretty collection of glass objects, including beaded-glass pagoda wall sconces, were chosen for their glittery, reflective quality. For the entrance hall, Mario wanted a complete absence of color. Ethereal silver tea-paper-covered walls and gray-painted Regency consoles convey Old Hollywood glamour.

ABOVE *A silk taffeta floral from Brunschwig & Fils and checked curtains in pinks and greens inject a fresh prettiness. An oval mirror strategically hung over a japanned Queen Anne bureau bookcase brings the eye up and emphasizes the vertical.*

RIGHT *Mario mirrored the wall behind the sofa in mercury glass to expand the room visually and to bring the city views right into the apartment. A painting by Russian artist Ivan Godlevsky hangs above.*

LEFT *The decorator warmed up a dark wood-paneled room into this pickled knotty pine library. Mario comments, "I like light libraries. This is a tiny little room. The warm pecan color of the paneling makes it cozy."*

BELOW *Mario ingeniously tented the dining room in an apple green batik-style print to conceal the couple's storage of crystal and china as the apartment had no extra closets or cupboards. "Because of the topiary trees, you feel you're in an orangery."*

The Empire State Building, visible from the southern window, inspired the profile of the mirrored bedposts in the master bedroom. Mrs. Ross's love of blue and white played out in a mixture of patterns unified by lavender walls. Blue gauze studded with white stars inside the bed's canopy creates the effect of looking up at the sky.

ABOVE *Mario designed the Deco-inspired bathroom with walls mirrored in four-inch strips. The white-with-black-border marble floor maintains the colorless palette. The revolving vanity chair was copied from the Duchess of Windsor's.*

61

Hilary and Wilbur Ross Pied-à-Terre

New York, New York

When the Rosses moved to this duplex penthouse, everything from their previous residence could be reused as is, and, as a testament to Mario's genius for furniture arrangement, only an additional low table was needed to supplement the existing furnishings for the 36-foot-long double-height living room, originally a ballroom. Even the same blue dhurrie rug fit perfectly. Mario opted for an apple green background—instead of eggplant, which was used in the entrance hall (above)—to infuse the walls with sunlight pouring through the generously scaled French doors. That a new wall color could work as gorgeously as the former is a result of Mario's expert color sense. As Mrs. Ross enthuses, "Mario has an artist's eye."

ABOVE *Though the living room was already distinguished with a barrel-vaulted ceiling, the decorator brought in further architectural details, including the overdoor pediments and dentil molding.*

PRECEDING SPREAD *The clients are passionate collectors of modern and contemporary art. "I like to mix everything up. Different periods, different artists—it makes everything more interesting," says Mrs. Ross.*

OPPOSITE *Mario again opted for a tented dining room to help diffuse the strong light; it also wonderfully absorbs sound. Three octagonal tables are set for large dinner parties, and for even larger ones, a long tabletop is placed over all three. Mario keeps the room from becoming too grand with sisal carpeting.*

ABOVE *The card room's faux tortoiseshell-painted walls give instant drama and personality to a small room that is mainly used as a passageway to the terrace.*

BELOW *A 2,000-square-foot terrace overlooking Carnegie Hall wraps around the apartment and is generously furnished for entertaining. Mario conceived a pagodalike pavilion incorporating a working fireplace and seating.*

OPPOSITE *Two small bedrooms were merged to make a library installed with pickled knotty pine paneling similar to that in the Rosses' previous apartment. The ceiling is covered in squares of Gracie gold-leaf paper on the diagonal.*

Upper East Side Duplex Penthouse *New York, New York*

Evoking the elegant sparseness and lightness of Swedish neoclassicism, Mario enrobed his client's sun-flooded living room in creamy white. The space is kept airy with a firmly curated collection of painted antiques, ivory upholstery, and a bare travertine floor. The decorator selected relatively simple striped taffeta festoon curtains.

A double-sided sofa allows for multiple seating groups. Myriad textures and finishes keep the blanc-de-blanc palette rich and complex.

LEFT *The creamy white continues in the book-lined library, made cozier with a silver papered ceiling and an antique Aubusson carpet overlaid on wall-to-wall sisal. A parcel-gilt Swedish Empire table balances the St. Thomas sofa opposite.*

ABOVE *The dining room is tented and shirred in striped silk fabric. A Swedish chandelier hangs over the round table. The floor is painted to resemble a marble inlaid floor.*

Patricia Altschul Residence, Fifth Avenue Maisonette

New York, New York

When client Patricia Altschul confided to Mario that she was contemplating buying a two-bedroom apartment once belonging to Sister Parish, Mario assured her it was the right decision even if it was in need of a major overhaul. The decorator recalls, "Sister had a great sense of color. One time I was here, the living room was eggplant; another time, blue; and another time, beige." The first room of the apartment was conceived as a dining hall just as in Sister's day. Taking the Chinese Pavilion at Drottningholm as a departure point, the chocolate brown room was painted with Chinese-style dado and borders to look like a bamboo tent. The ceiling was wallpapered and then painted with a fretwork border and spandrels. A corner banquette, flanked by blackamoor side tables once belonging to Evangeline Bruce, opens up the room and provides extra seating for dinner parties at the round marble-top table with whimsical tree-trunk base. The red concave chinoiserie side cabinet is from Mario's collection for John Widdicomb.

LEFT *The client asked Mario for high glamour and sparkle. He responded by covering the wall in a shimmery silver paper from Gracie, giving the room an ethereal, romantic glow. The decorator explains, "The silver paper makes the room sing. It also keeps it open and airy." Sensuous touches of gilt and raspberry counterbalance the coolness. "No one does curtains like Mario," says Mrs. Altschul. "He took three shades of mauve silk, sewed them side by side, edged them in crystal fringe and backed them with lavender silk taffeta. It creates this magical optical illusion of waves of color—it's extraordinary." The marble faux fireplace was installed to give the room a natural focal point. On one of their shopping trips to London, designer and client found the fantastical Chinese Chippendale overmantel mirror. An eighteenth-century red bureau bookcase acts as a base for all the pale tones.*

FOLLOWING SPREAD *Mario kept the antiqued glass panels behind the sofa originally put in by Sister. The pair of Regency gilt-metal hanging shelves display a collection of porcelain vegetables.*

LEFT *For the client's bedroom, Mario went all out with Colefax and Fowler floral chintz curtains and bed hangings—their edges pinked and set off by a coral pink underlayer. A hand-painted cushion by George Oakes on the chaise longue is another nod to the decorator's idol and mentor, John Fowler. Mrs. Altschul's collection of antique English and French needlework hangs on the walls, including a dog picture previously owned by Jacqueline Onassis. Claret grosgrain ribbon outlines the room. "It made such a difference—Mario is always thinking of how to enhance things down to the finest detail. He once painted a straight-forward bouillotte lampshade in stripes!"*

BELOW *The master bathroom's Directoire scheme is softened by shell pink Pompeian-style murals and antique creamware plates arranged on the walls.*

Aileen Mehle Residence

New York, New York

Friend and client Aileen Mehle, whose society column *Suzy* was a must-read for the in crowd for decades, turned to Mario when she moved into an apartment featuring a double-height ballroom in a 1903 Horace Trumbauer-designed townhouse. A previous tenant and prodigious entertainer, Fiat heiress Suni Agnelli, had covered the walls in a vibrant, pulse-racing russet floral and had installed bleacherlike tiered sofas at one end. The decorator covered the walls in a pleasing salmon Indian silk woven with tulips, removed the stepped-back sofas, and designed a new graceful curving staircase up to the second level. The client's collection of nineteenth-century paintings hangs on the walls.

LEFT *The Scalamandré blue cotton-covered walls feature butterflies and magnolia blossoms, and are a remnant from previous resident Suni Agnelli. Mario reconfigured Mehle's curtains from her last apartment by adding the Turkish valance.*

PRECEDING SPREAD *One walks through the dining room to enter the living room. Mario ingeniously softened the transition of ceiling heights by tenting the space in a celadon green and white striped silk taffeta. Rope passementerie from Scalamandré dresses up the ceiling.*

Fifth Avenue Apartment

New York, New York

A Texas client sought out Mario to put his imprimatur on her New York pied-à-terre. Yellow and blue, one of his favorite color combinations, are paired together in the large living room overlooking Central Park, accented by corals and greens. A pennant valance at the wall of windows evokes a tented setting and emphasizes that the views are part of the interior. A French linen velvet dhurrie covers the floor.

ABOVE *Mario selected the striking deep orange hand-painted Chinese paper from Gracie to offset the graphic zigzag-stained floor done by the previous owner.*

RIGHT and FOLLOWING SPREAD *A dining room didn't make sense for the client's needs, so it was reimagined as a library, luxuriously tented with a Prussian blue paisley print. As with the entrance hall, the leopard carpet balances the boldness of the wallcovering. Tortoiseshell-stained bamboo shades behind the curtains enhance the exotic mood while filtering the bright southern light.*

LEFT *The master bedroom is striéed and glazed a pale lime green, emphasized by lime green and cream striped curtains. A 1930s-style silvered shell-back chair injects screen-siren glamour.*

ABOVE *The guest bedroom is covered in pale blue moiré wallpaper with a forget-me-not blue Colefax and Fowler linen floral used for the curtains and the bedskirt of the* lit à la polonaise.

Mariah Carey Residence

New York, New York

When celebrated songstress Mariah Carey bought a triplex in an old bank building in Tribeca, she turned to Mario to design the glamorous apartment of her dreams. It was a complete gut-renovation, with the decorator supervising the placement of walls and doorways. The streamlined neoclassicism of the Deco style inspired many of the architectural details including the paneled silver-leaf doors—similar to ones in Mario's house growing up—and stepped ceiling in the apricot glazed entrance hall. A bronze-inset marble floor and Moderne lantern evoke the high style of a Rogers-Astaire movie set. Room schemes often begin with selecting the right fabric. After showing Ms. Carey hundreds of swatches, he realized flowers weren't for her. Instead, lustrous champagne and apricot satins and silks befitting a screen siren of the 1930s were the look she was after. As the apartment is mainly enjoyed in the evening after long hours working in the studio, soft romantic lighting was designed for the living room.

99

ABOVE *A round table, covered in chocolate brown satin, divides the long living room. "People rarely use dining rooms anymore," says the decorator.*

LEFT *The L-shaped living room—occupying almost the entire lowest floor of the residence—is demarcated into three separate areas for entertaining and dining. An espresso-stained floor anchors the pastel-colored room.*

LEFT *While the bookshelf niches continue the apartment's Deco styling, Mario installed a traditional fireplace to give the master bedroom an Old New York charm. The only floral to be found anywhere is the amethyst and oyster gray Bennison silk print.*

BELOW *Ms. Carey's preference for soft, pale colors determined the room's palette: lavender walls, a pale pink ceiling, and creamy white carpeting. The elaborate curtains are made of creamy white silk satin with lavender lining, with floral silk shades underneath.*

Cathy Hardwick Residence *New York, New York*

When fashion designer Cathy Hardwick moved from her former Mario-decorated apartment into a larger loftlike one in the same building, there was no question she would ask the designer to Buattafy it. After reconfiguring walls so there was a proper progression of rooms and putting in appropriate moldings and architectural detail, Mario was ready to create new settings for Hardwick's collections. The living room of Hardwick's previous apartment (pictured above) was glazed deep hunter green and was more square in proportion—but other than a new wall color, a slight reworking of the curtains, and a new furniture plan, all of her previous pieces were able to be reused. In keeping with Mario's philosophy that entrance halls should have an elegant formality, he had artist Robert Jackson paint the floor with trompe-l'oeil marble, Adam-style decoration inspired by the grand entrance of Kedleston Hall. A small figure of a Boston Terrier under the demilune console table adds a note of whimsy.

BELOW *Mario and client Cathy Hardwick both share a passion for the English style. Hardwick's scarlet japanned Queen Anne bureau bookcase is similar to one the decorator has.*

LEFT and FOLLOWING SPREAD *Mario decided on a paler background—Alan Campbell white-on-white striped wallpaper—for the new light-filled living room. The needlepoint rug, upholstery, and windowpane-plaid taffeta curtains, slightly altered, were all in the previous apartment.*

107

Mario Buatta Residence

New York, New York

In 1976 Mario moved into his current apartment in a 1929 neo-Georgian doublewide townhouse built by noted architects Cross and Cross for Martha and George Whitney. While the rooms have essentially remained the same over the years, they have continued to evolve and "grow like a garden" as Mario has added to his collections. His octagonal entrance hall, also used as a dining room, is the house's original reception hall. Apricot glazed walls set off his collection of Delft and Chinese export blue and white porcelain. "The peach pink color warms the blue and white and gives my pieces a whole new dimension; it crisps the white." An octagonal center table skirted in geranium red silk references the Villa Foscari, also known as La Malcontenta, which so impressed the decorator the first time he saw it as a student. The dining chairs once belonged to fashion designer Norman Norell, and the chandelier came out of Nancy Lancaster's country house, Haseley Court.

Mario's living room, designed as the original house's library, is glazed in three shades of lime green and creamy white, with a faux-sisal painted floor. Over the sofa hangs Mario's collection of dog paintings. He bought his first one, the painting of three spaniels on the upper right, in 1963. Mario often jokes, "These paintings are my ancestors. Seriously, I love dogs. I don't have a dog because I have such a busy schedule, but I love viewing them on the wall." To the left of the sofa is a blue and white French screen, which he would hide behind to overhear prospective clients' first impressions.

113

Another view of the living room. Hanging over the faux-bamboo Chippendale settee is a painting referencing the signing of the treaty that ended the Boxer Rebellion. The two dogs represent Great Britain and France, and the pagoda in the background signifies China.

114

RIGHT *The decorator's New York garden of porcelain tulips is displayed in a red japanned bureau bookcase. The same Floral Bouquet curtains have hung in all six of Mario's apartments. "Each time, they were added on to at the bottom or the sides—they're like patchwork curtains now, but I've never tired of the chintz."*

BELOW *A collection of japanned, penwork, lacquered, and painted boxes are displayed as a tower in a corner.*

ABOVE *A birthday card painted by Tom Morrow is a comic rendition of what it would be like to be in a dog's house with a collection of Mario portraits.*

BELOW *The November 1980 cover of* House & Garden *highlights a tablescape.*

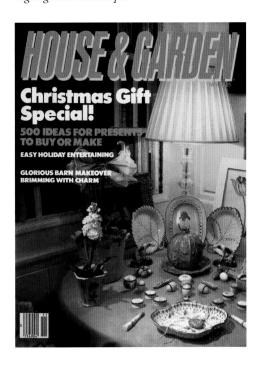

Park Avenue Bedroom

New York, New York

This master bedroom captures the sun with its brightly glazed celery green walls. The floor is painted in a blue and white geometric design to visually expand the space with sprays of varying flora and fauna scattered within the circles' reserves. Mario keeps the room restful by opting for simple snow-white point-d'esprit bed hangings. The zigzag apple green and white curtains with Turkish valance enhance the windows. Over the fireplace, a remote-controlled painting moves to reveal a flat-screen television with the push of a button.

Fifth Avenue
Pied-à-Terre *New York, New York*

Decades after completing this project, Mario reflects, "Even though I decorated this twenty years ago, it's hard to say when it was done. I like to think my work has a timeless look to it." Before even considering colors or fabrics, he first set about making all the necessary alterations to the apartment's layout and architectural details—with the help of architect John Murray, then a partner at Ferguson, Murray & Shamamian—so that the spaces would function as comfortably as possible. "Together we decided what to do—bring out the bones, raise the height of the doors, open up the windows to embrace the magical view of the park, create a badly needed flow, remove certain walls, and shift others forward." For the windowless entrance hall, Robert Jackson painted the pastoral mural, which depicts the owners' country houses. "It's soft and romantic—it gives you a wonderful feeling when you walk in." In the lemon yellow living room, striped silk curtains visually increase the ceiling height.

The clients' American
Impressionist pictures
beautifully echo Mario's
painterly color scheme
of sky blue, raspberry,
sunburst yellow,
and lettuce green.

123

"It's important to have day rooms and night rooms," instructs Mario. He creates an evening one here for his clients by installing mahogany paneling designed by Murray in the library, which is also used for dining and watching television. An antique paisley Bessarabian carpet delineates the main seating group. Gold-leaf tea paper warms the ceiling.

LEFT *"The master bedroom's canopy bed almost becomes a separate room within a room,"* notes the decorator. *A Scalamandré floral chintz harmonizes with apricot silk plaid curtains against pale pink walls. To create the illusion of a picture window, two windows are visually united with a Stone valance in the same material as the curtains.*

BELOW *The guest bedroom is upholstered in a flax and white stripe with coordinating curtains. The bamboo four-poster bed is dressed in a Clarence House animal print. The carpet is a Colefax and Fowler design with octagon and leaf motifs.*

Upper East Side Pied-à-Terre *New York, New York*

Mario always gives great thought to the first impression an entrance hall makes. For the South American owners of this apartment, Mario had a tropical landscape painted by Robert Jackson to remind them of home. A trompe-l'oeil balustrade and faux-marble painted parquet floor further evoke the feeling of walking onto a veranda. Many architectural details were added throughout the apartment, and all the contents, including fine English and Irish antiques, were purchased especially— but gradually—for the space. Mario warns against the "room out of a box" syndrome and takes great pains to make his spaces look like they have naturally evolved—even a room with all newly acquired pieces.

LEFT *"If you have a long rectangular room, a corner sofa
is a wonderful way to open up the space,"* says Mario.
A coromandel screen rounds off the corner and adds height.

BELOW *The living room was glazed with pea green stripes.
The espresso-ground Bessarabian rug sets off the pale palette.
The decorator purposely selected a mixture of prints
and paintings for the room to give the feel that they
had been hung over a period of years.*

ABOVE *A newly installed marble fireplace is the focal point of the room.
However, Mario wasn't compelled to center a seating group around it.
"It's not that big a room. It's a standard New York City prewar apartment,
but what's great is you can seat three groups of four very comfortably."*

FOLLOWING SPREAD *After living in the space for a year, the clients
realized they didn't need a dedicated dining room, so Mario reimagined
it as a library with maps and a handsome George III mahogany bookcase.
A round mahogany table is used for dining.*

Manor House *Tulsa, Oklahoma*

Long-time clients commissioned Mario and Ferguson & Shamamian Architects to design a new 8,000-square-foot residence that looked like it had evolved over generations. Lofty oak-beamed ceilings throughout give a rustic elegance to the house's interior. The entrance hall's biscuit white walls are counterbalanced by russet curtains. An octagonal table, covered in a Meyer-lemon-colored cloth and harkening to La Malcontenta, centers the space. The great room features a 23-foot-high ceiling and creamy white walls. Six sets of French doors look out to terraces. Norman-style fireplaces anchor each end of the room.

RIGHT *This stonewall outdoor room off the entrance hall is one of Mario's favorites: "It's a wonderful room at night and during the day; it's a very comfortable place to read a book outdoors."*

BELOW *Mario masterfully arranges multiple seating groups, like this one around the fireplace, so that even an immense room feels intimate.*

138

LEFT *The floral-embroidered linen-draped* lit à la polonaise *picturesquely commands the master bedroom. The ivory white floor is painted with scattered green leaves and flowers, and the lilac walls are embellished with trompe-l'oeil trelliswork to continue the romantic mood. The crystal chandelier—shaped like a hot air balloon—strikes a note of whimsy.*

BELOW *A Manuel Canovas blue and white linen toile of pomegranates is used throughout a guest bedroom.*

141

Georgian House *Manila, Philippines*

After years of admiring Mario's work from afar, a client from the Philippines hired the designer to first work on a New York pied-à-terre and later this house in Manila to which he was adding an extension. "He had loved my apartment and wanted my living room. He had already painted his the same pineapple yellow and copied my French screen." Mario took the living room in hand by adding more seating groups, such as a large corner banquette—a favorite Buatta-ism to open up a space. "It was a large room and needed serious cozying up." He also arranged furniture, objects, and paintings "like a garden" so that the eye travels up and down, and added a blue and white floral needlepoint rug.

ABOVE *Another view of the living room: a portrait of the client's mother anchors the wall over the sofa, which is flanked by two copies of Mario's own blue and white French screen.*

OPPOSITE *Mario had the double-height study painted in faux tortoise by a local artist to rein in the large scale of the room.*

144

LEFT *The hallway leading to the library is part of the new extension. The floors are painted with a faux-marble black and white checkerboard.*

RIGHT and BELOW *The new library received Georgian-style paneling made of knotty pine with a pickled finish. La Portugaise in green— a bold nineteenth-century print from Brunschwig & Fils— covers the club chairs. The back-to-back sofas center the room and create four seating groups.*

ABOVE *Mario designed the ceiling shape after the lines of a tent, in this ticking-draped dressing room inspired by Napoleon's. Closets are concealed behind all four walls.*

OPPOSITE *The octagonal dining room is painted in three shades of apple green, with trompe-l'oeil tassels embellishing the plates hung on the wall. Billy Baldwin-style armchairs from DeAngelis are covered in blue and white checked slipcovers.*

149

Fred Woolworth Residence

New York, New York

This plum project came with refined ingredients: a Fifth Avenue prewar apartment that was once the bedroom floor of the client's cousin Barbara Hutton's triplex, and a fine collection of English furniture and American paintings. For the light-flooded paneled living room, Mario decided on three shades of lemon for the walls; the rest of the apartment continues the pastel colorscape. Woolworth's preference for a more contemporary feel prompted a more restrained use of pattern. The designer's genius for arrangement was essential for the living room. "Perhaps because the rooms had been mainly informal and private in the original scheme of things, we had some slightly eccentric proportions to deal with. In the living room, the fireplace is off-center, and there's an entrance door at the south end. I avoided the usual static arrangement of chairs around the fireplace and opened everything out toward the center of the room."

Sutton Place
Dining Room *New York, New York*

To refresh this dining room, Mario glazed the walls apricot—a color that makes everyone look their best—and installed beige and white striped festoon shades with deep tan edging to allow for the dramatic river views. A pair of round brass-banded dining tables are accompanied by a set of leather-upholstered Directoire side chairs. Sisal carpeting, a Buatta favorite to prevent dining rooms from getting too grand, covers the floor.

Fifth Avenue Pied-à-Terre *New York, New York*

The client, a Filipino businessman, had long admired Mario's work and even replicated elements of the decorator's own living room for his Manila house (on which Mario would consult years later; see pages 142–149). This one-bedroom apartment was their first collaboration. As the L-shaped living room was used mainly in the evening, Mario glazed the walls a glossy evergreen and used brown-ground Colefax and Fowler chintz for the curtains, club chair, and ottoman. Folding screens painted the same green as the walls were positioned so that a dining area could be set apart when desired.

ABOVE *White and beige linen covers the walls and dresses the bed in a riff on a tented room. Deep tan grosgrain banding adds architectural distinction. A Rose Cumming leaf print for the bed's headboard and skirt soften the tailored scheme.*

LEFT *Moldings were added throughout the apartment, and in the Pompeian red library, bookcases were built in. The client's burgeoning collection of dogs—a passion shared with Mario—is on display.*

157

Blair House *Washington, D.C.*

When an extensive restoration of Blair House, the presidential guest quarters, was undertaken in 1982, appropriations were included for a redecoration program. Curator Clement E. Conger selected Mark Hampton and Mario, as the country's foremost interior designers, to take on the 112-room project, ultimately completed in 1988. The Federal-period Blair House had grown to include the adjacent Blair-Lee House, a press wing, and a new wing for the Primary Suite, seven rooms that were designated for visiting heads of state. The designers divvied up the rooms, with Mario taking the Blair-Lee House and the new Primary Suite. Both agreed that the decor should be referential to historical Anglo-American design, but it should foremost be considered as a welcoming residence with up-to-date comforts. The designers had one opportunity to view the existing furnishings in storage and then had to rely on their memories as they developed their furniture plans. The entrance hall of Blair-Lee (opposite) was covered in a French nineteenth-century tobacco-ground Mauny paper.

Mario had the Dillon Room's historic hand-painted Chinese wallpaper cleaned and restored before it was rehung. The wallpaper inspired the room's lively color scheme, which fused in the striped silk curtains under hand-carved giltwood pelmets.

161

ABOVE *For the Blair-Lee dining room Mario decided on a crisp blue and white scheme inspired by the Lee family's collection of porcelain displayed there. Period paneling from a Frelinghuysen family house in New Jersey was installed in the room. On the chair seats is needlepoint worked by the wives of the cabinet during the Kennedy administration.*

LEFT *Mario fought for and won his wish to paint the Truman Study—named for President Harry S. Truman, who was almost assassinated in this room— a patriotic red. A Brunschwig & Fils tree-of-life cretonne is used for the curtains. The mantel, one of a pair that are reputed to be by Stanford White, was previously in Mrs. Theodore Roosevelt's White House bedroom.*

For the main sitting room and all the other rooms of the Primary Suite, fine antique furniture from a New York townhouse was donated. Conger and Mario visited the house and handpicked appropriate pieces. Margaret Thatcher was the first visiting head of state to stay in the suite. President-elect George H. W. Bush and his wife, Barbara, also stayed in the suite before his inauguration. Mario wrote Mrs. Bush a note imploring her to protect the porcelain from her grandchildren. She teasingly replied, "Don't worry—we're playing football right now with the china, but we'll make sure we repair everything with Elmer's glue so you'd never know!"

165

ABOVE *A Chinese-design striped print,
which complements the Regency tester bed,
is used throughout a secondary bedroom
in the Primary Suite.*

LEFT *Mario delivers full-blown chintz
for the Primary Suite's master bedroom.
He had the missing headboard remade
and the bedposts repainted to coordinate
with the floral print.*

Dailey and Gordon Pattee
Residence *New York, New York*

The Pattees commissioned Mario to decorate their Park
Avenue triplex after being smitten by the *eau de nil* living
room he created for the 1987 Kips Bay Show House. The
pale yellow tones of the entrance hall's chinoiserie mural
painted by Robert Jackson belie the riot of color in the rooms
beyond, including apple green, plum, and peacock blue in
the library (at right). "I gave them two day rooms and two
night rooms," says the designer. Antique chairs for the
couple's children are grouped in front of the fireplace in the
library, ready for a Christmas card portrait. A yellow-ground
chintz from Brunschwig & Fils is used for the curtains and
a club chair. A decorative salmon taffeta sash suspends the
old master work above the mantel. "I used the sash here
because the painting was the focal point of the room."

168

RIGHT *The morning room was painted the same pale green as the show-house room the clients first admired. Mario refers to the chintz as "a wonderful garden print."*

BELOW *The ice blue dining room painted with trelliswork is off the entrance hall (above). Sugared-almond striped silk curtains were kept unlined to allow as much light to stream in as possible.*

ABOVE and LEFT *The client wanted the living room to be green and burst into tears when she first saw the deep eggplant walls. Mario reassured her that she would love it once it was layered with all the sherbet-hued furnishings, and he was right. Bold black and gilt Regency furniture, such as the pair of Egyptian stools and the dolphin-form side table, balances the pastel palette. The client chose the large nineteenth-century Aubusson.*

LEFT *The four-poster bed in the master bedroom was specially designed for the client. Lavender papered walls, blue and white paisley carpet, and "a pretty, pretty chintz" provided a romantic, soft background.*

BELOW *A star mirror over the fireplace announces the more relaxed mood of this upstairs sitting room, off a large terrace.*

Nancy and Frank S. Benson, Jr. Residence *Columbus, Ohio*

After the Bensons were charmed by this 1929 Normandy-style stucco house located in an historic section of Columbus, they sought Mario's expertise to make the interiors as entrancing as the exterior. With the assistance of architect Jack Coble, the designer enlarged the main reception rooms and added bay windows to let in much-needed light, all the while taking care to preserve the house's facade and floor plan. In the entrance hall, artist Robert Jackson painted a chinoiserie mural in the style of Jean-Baptiste Pillement—into the landscape went all the clients' children and houses, and, with a touch of humor, the husband coming home on a tightrope. "Entrances are terribly important because they make the first impression. This was originally a dark and dead space. The fantasy of walking through a forest makes people stop and stare, wondering what surprises are waiting in the rooms beyond." When Mr. Benson first saw the decoration, he jested, "There is so much faux in here, I'm going to faux up!"

ABOVE and BELOW *A Chinese lantern designed by Mario hangs from the trompe-l'oeil skylight painted with bamboo framework. The mural's fresh blues and greens brighten up the space.*

RIGHT *A newly installed bay window behind the sofa opens up the living room. As usual, Mario gave great thought to the color flow of the house: "I tried to make each room a surprise. I wanted to see a slight change in tone and texture—like the excitement of looking into a flower that's about to open and seeing all the colors." A Rose Cumming chintz covers the sofa and one chair.*

LEFT *The paneled library is a cozy room
that the couple and their family use as a retreat.
Their fine collection of American paintings
by Alice Schille commands the walls.
The sofa and club chair are covered in
a Pierre Frey printed cotton paisley.*

BELOW *A small sunroom has sky blue walls
with trellis decoration. The floors are painted
to look like flagstone with flowers popping
through the spaces between the stones.*

FOLLOWING SPREAD *Wicker furnishings and
luxurious massings of foliage and flowers give
the newly built pool house pavilion, designed by
Jack Coble, a tropical feel. Pastel fabrics and
shell pink walls complement the brightly colored
dhurrie covering the limestone floor.*

181

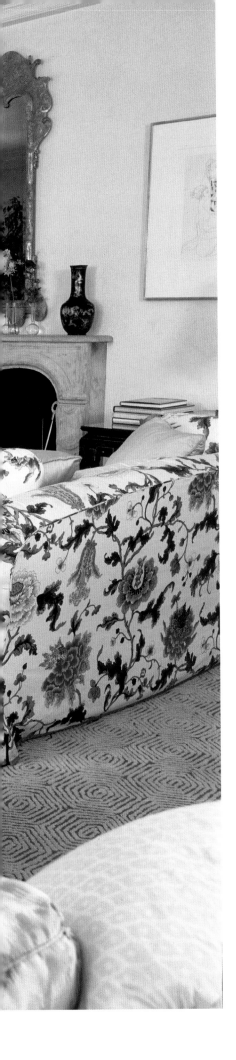

Park Avenue Duplex *New York, New York*

Mario first worked for this client's mother in 1969 and has continued to decorate for various members of the family ever since. For the couple's city residence, which is filled with their important art collection, Mario enrobed the living room in a symphony of ivory white. The glazed walls, quilted curtains, and woven wool rug add texture to the eggshell scheme. A gilt gesso Queen Anne mirror over the fireplace adds glitter, while the bursting pinks and purples of Athos, the Brunschwig & Fils chintz on the sofa, keep it lively. A large Morris Louis color-field painting asserts itself on a wall of the living room.

185

LEFT *Mario often incorporates potted trees (fishtail palms are a particular favorite) to bring an outdoor element into a room as well as to add a varying height. "You don't want a room to look like a flat sea—as a garden is landscaped with plants of different heights, so should your room."*

BELOW *A painting by Jack Beal hangs over the sofa in the cranberry red-glazed library. The coffee table is stacked with books and magazines—signs of a lived-in interior, which the decorator wholeheartedly endorses.*

ABOVE *A detail of the table festively set for a dinner party.*

LEFT *An apricot and grass green scheme sets off the large forest scene by Neil Welliver in the dining room. "It's like dining on a patio at sunset," says the client. A mirrored frieze gives the room a floating effect. All the textiles were custom-made for the room, including the floral print seat upholstery by Tillett and the lilac and apricot–striped curtains.*

Mario does a naive version of his English-country-house look in this pale pink bedroom. The floor's painted decoration is inspired by an antique American quilt.

191

Central Park West Tower Apartment

New York, New York

The decoration of this sprawling five-level apartment garnered Mario his first *Architectural Digest* cover. The first floor comprised the entrance hall, living room (pictured above and at right), dining room, library, and kitchen. Everything was acquired for the apartment. The client loved his lemon yellow living room with accents of blue so much that he began his own collection of blue and white porcelain.

ABOVE *The living room looks out to dazzling city views.*
Striped curtains are edged on the bias.

RIGHT *An L-shaped sofa is the foundation*
of one of the room's four seating groups.

The dining room was hand-painted by Robert Jackson with Chinese flowering trees. The formal elegance of the eighteenth-century English mahogany furniture is played down by the sisal carpet. Dinner for twelve is more intimate at two tables for six.

196

ABOVE and RIGHT *Mario gave his clients two night rooms.*
The husband's study (above) is covered in tortoiseshell vinyl.
The red lacquered library (right), the first room one sees
when entering the apartment, shows all the layers of a lived-in room.

OPPOSITE *The bedroom is upholstered in a pink seaweed print with matching curtains to de-emphasize the off-center placement of the windows. The shirred tambour bed curtains are hung from the ceiling, allowing for a dramatic and picturesque scale. The floor is carpeted with the decorator's flowering-trellis design from Stark.*

BELOW *The tower's fourth floor features arched windows on three exposures and a fireplace on the fourth wall. Mario raised the floor five feet so the views were maximized. Even so altered, the ceiling soars at twenty feet.*

Upper East Side
Townhouse Library *New York, New York*

For the 2006 Kips Bay Show House held in a fifty-foot-wide limestone townhouse at 4 East 75th Street, Mario's departure point was a linen fern print, Felce in ecru, from Old World Weavers. He drew out the moss green from the print for the velvet-covered walls. "The dark walls are a rich background for everything to stand out against," remarks the decorator. A gold tea-paper-covered ceiling adds luminosity, while strokes of brilliant red and butter yellow keep the scheme cheerful.

ABOVE *Blue and white porcelain vases on brackets make
for a dynamic arrangement and keep the eye moving.
The decorator warms up even his fantasy rooms with the
effects of everyday life: framed pictures, a carafe of water,
and a basket of magazines.*

OPPOSITE *Mario's fondness for dogs is on display with the canine
portraits hung throughout the room. On the tartan ottoman
is a small throw pillow needlepointed with the saying:
"Missing! Fisherman-Husband and Dog. Reward for Dog."*

Central Park West Bedroom *New York, New York*

Mario says that the theme for this master bedroom in the newly unveiled Time Warner Center, "Under the Rainbow," was sparked by his seeing a rainbow over Central Park when he first visited the room. While prismatic rays of light inspired the cascading striped silk taffeta curtains on the bed and at the windows, the sweeping views of the park were also on his mind. He asked painter Haleh Atabeigi to render potted trees in each corner so one has the feeling of being in a park. The room, which started off as a white box, was given moldings and a decorative fireplace to provide a focal point. The mirrored screen from Niermann Weeks brings light and extended views of the park into the room.

206

Conservatory Landing

New York, New York

To celebrate the twenty-fifth anniversary of the Kips Bay Show House in 1997, the designers from the event's first year reconvened under the roof of a Park Avenue townhouse. Mario's space was a staircase landing that he transformed into a fantasy garden planted with painted, carved, and real flora. Artist Robert Jackson painted whimsical chinoiserie and architectural elements on the orchid pink walls. The floral trellis carpet expands the space visually. The sense of a room building up over time is captured with the nineteenth-century amethyst crystal chandelier, which wears its replaced flute regally—in an exuberant cranberry. Foxglove, hydrangea, and grape hyacinth—Mario's favorite flower—screen the staircase balustrade.

209

ABOVE *The landing becomes a dreamscape as the eye deciphers what is faux and what is real. The neoclassical overdoor tympanum was painted by Robert Jackson with a blue and white Delft garniture.*

OPPOSITE *Green-painted carved wooden palms originally made for Elsie de Wolfe echo the room's existing Ionic pilasters. A French baker's table is covered in moss and topped with a Gothic-style birdcage.*

Barbara Walters Sitting Room

New York, New York

Mario was asked to participate in the *Traditional Home* "Built for Women"
show house benefiting The Breast Cancer Research Foundation. Each of the
eleven suites of rooms was dedicated to a notable woman and Mario's was
acclaimed journalist and client Barbara Walters. Walters has joked that the
first morning she awoke in her newly decorated apartment, she at once saw
his face—as Mario had put a framed photograph of himself on her nightstand.
For the show house, he created an eggplant-glazed sitting room for the
hardworking newswoman to enjoy in the evenings. Ivory carpeting and plenty
of down-filled upholstered seating make the room soft and cosseting.

Walters's affinity for American paintings
inspired the pictures chosen for the room.
"Mario has the greatest color sense I've ever seen,"
Walters has said.

Bedroom *New York, New York*

The star of every Buatta bedroom is the bed, invariably of impressive scale and romantically dressed and curtained. "The most macho of men will get into one of these beds and not want to get out," jokes the designer. For this Kips Bay Show House room, the decorator opted for a *lit à la polonaise* hung with gauzy white linen, a foil for Melanie, a floral and gingham striped sheeting from his own collection for Revman, which he used for the headboard, bedskirt, comforter, and the room's curtains. Three shades of lemon yellow warm up the room's northern light. Creamware plates flank the oval mirror above the fireplace.

216

Townhouse Living Room

New York, New York

Mario's show-house rooms have always been feted, and this one for the 1987 Kips Bay benefit was no exception. The decorator received the ultimate compliment when a new client saw his room, at a stately thirty-five-feet long, and acquired it for her California residence—with the exception of the blue and white French screen, brought from the decorator's own home. Ebullient striped festoon curtains preside over the windows, and eighteenth- and nineteenth-century porcelains fill the bookshelves.

Townhouse Sitting Room New York, New York

Luscious cherry red-glazed walls offer a brilliant backdrop for the chinoiserie chintz Le Lac from Brunschwig & Fils in this sitting room designed for the Kips Bay Show House. With such rich, full-bodied hues, natural light is immaterial to illuminating the room. Antique dog portraits, many from the decorator's own walls, hang over the sofa. An American quilt covers a round table, and a folding screen covered with nineteenth-century wallpaper samples is positioned in a corner. On opening night, Mario, standing behind the door, overheard Sister Parish remark to Albert Hadley, "He has one of everything I've ever owned in this room!"

Townhouse Bedroom

New York, New York

It is this iconic bedroom created for the 1984 Kips Bay Show House that earned Mario the moniker "The Prince of Chintz" from news reporter Chauncey Howell. Two shades of lavender glaze the walls in stripes and provide a foil for the piquant blue of Verrieres from Brunschwig & Fils. "This blue fabric is a favorite of mine. But every time I've used it, I've always had to put it against white or pale blue walls. No one would ever let me place it against lavender walls. People have never understood the combination of blue and lavender, which is often seen on English and Chinese porcelain and Delftware. It is so pretty. But because this was a showhouse room, I was able to do exactly what I wanted to." The bed's canopy is suspended from the ceiling and dressed in translucent handkerchief linen edged in a cotton bobble trim. A fantastical eighteenth-century stripped-pine chinoiserie mantelpiece, complete with mirror, balances the wall opposite the bed. *House Beautiful* editor Margaret Kennedy, who devoted the cover and seven pages to the room in the magazine, says, "If a particular room at a particular moment can define an era, this was it. Mario's blue and white bedroom seduced me the minute I walked onto the geometric carpeting. The genius of the room was that in the midst of muchness, the airiness of the white bed calmed it down, as did the pale lavender walls, which receded. At the height of America's obsession with English country style, Mario's interpretation was the best."

223

Sitting Room New York, New York

Plum walls were the dramatic backdrop for this sitting room in the first Kips Bay Show House, held in 1973. The room's admirers included Albert Hadley, who once said of the decorator, "Mario is not fashionable; he doesn't play that game. He has a great eye, great humor, and great knowledge." Eleanor Brown of McMillen was so taken by the room, she wanted to hire him. A pale blue-ground floral chintz and dhurrie rug soften the scheme. The plaid silk curtains help to bring in sun and light. The dog painting over the sofa is just one item taken from the decorator's own home.

224

ABOVE and RIGHT *A raspberry linen velvet oval ottoman,
copied from one of John Fowler's, sits before the fireplace.
The designer's preference for painted and lacquered
furniture is evident here. The Chippendale chinoiserie
mirror hangs above the room's original fireplace.*

Syracuse University Lubin House
Living Room *New York, New York*

Mario decided on a more contemporary approach for this show-house room. The walls were glazed café au lait to warm up the large room. The sherbet rainbow colors in the Robert Natkin painting over the sofa play out in the Colefax and Fowler floral print and soft pink upholstery. A multicolored chocolate brown-ground Portuguese carpet, custom-made by Stark, sets off the pastel tones. A nontraditional York Kennedy coffee table centers one seating group.

Paintings propped against the wall and an almost bare mantel reflect the restrained approach the decorator took with this room. Flanking the fireplace are the decorator's own Georgian-style tables, designed by Dorothy Draper for a Victorian house on Staten Island.

231

Townhouse Library *New York, New York*

This oval library at 1 East 94th Street was originally the dining room in the limestone townhouse redesigned by noted architect Cass Gilbert for himself in 1921. The neoclassical knotty pine paneling was the perfect backdrop for Mario's English-country-house style. The ceiling is covered in gold tea paper to add a warm glow, and canary yellow Regency-style linen curtains were hung over the French doors to intensify the northern light. A "Siamese sofa" in the center of the space neatly divides the room into two main seating groups. A fireplace anchors one end of the room.

A black eighteenth-century chinoiserie-decorated bureau bookcase dressed with colorful ceramics provides a focal point for the opposite end of the room. The decorator gauges scale and color by expertly mixing floral, plaid, and animal prints.

235

Master Bedroom *New York, New York*

"I call this room 'Separate Bedrooms,' because in their later years a lot of people really do have separate bedrooms. But it's done with a kind of whimsy. That's the point of the pillow needlepointed 'Tonight' on one side and 'Not Tonight' on the other. This is a very feminine room with layers and layers of fabric, all very soft and luxurious." Mario painted the high ceiling lavender to pull it in and used festoon curtains to emphasize the windows' height. All furniture and fabric are from the decorator's own lines. Shirred cotton named "Aileen's Melee" after his friend and client, *Suzy* columnist Aileen Mehle, hide a multitude of architectural flaws in this *Metropolitan Home* show-house room.

Library New York, New York

Deep claret walls provide a dramatic backdrop in a young couple's library. The designer recommends dark walls in a high-gloss finish to catch and reflect light. "When a room is dark, it's best to keep it a dark color, because it will never be bright. It would defy the light." The room's clear, confident colors make the traditional furnishings read as modern and in step with the abstract painting by Jonathan Edwards over the sofa.

Former Residence of Mario Buatta *New York, New York*

When this apartment was first published in 1970, many acclaimed the rooms for their highly personal and slightly rebellious retrograde, layered styling. His Dole pineapple yellow-glazed living room, a fresh interpretation of Nancy Lancaster's "buttah yeller," prompted countless requests from clients over the years to replicate his living room for them. His blue and white porcelain collection sings against the yellow and is arranged on brackets, shelves, and tabletops throughout the room. Mario's other nods to Colefax and Fowler style include the decorative blue silk sashes suspending the oval Chinese reverse-glass paintings and the blue and white Maltese-cross wool carpet, a favorite of Fowler's. When Mario showed Fowler the published photos of the room, Fowler quipped, "My dear boy, if you are going to copy me, you should do a better job." To which Mario riposted, "I wasn't copying you, sir. I was *inspired* by you."

OPPOSITE and RIGHT (top and bottom)
"This room needs a chintz repellent spray!" a design colleague once jested upon entering the room. Mario's beloved Floral Bouquet chintz curtains were brought from his previous apartment and will follow him to his next. Every surface is an opportunity for display, and Mario excels at the art of arrangement—while making it look effortless. "Everything in the room has a story, in the sense that it means something to me," the designer told Connoisseur *magazine.*

ABOVE, BELOW, and RIGHT *A Regency four-poster bed dressed in an Indian cretonne commands the decorator's cherry red bedroom. An American red and white quilt is that touch of "humble elegance" that keeps the room from skewing too formal. A large white-painted bookcase designed by Mario anchors the wall opposite the bed and adds architectural distinction.*

244

Gates Davison Residence

New York, New York

Davison was one of Mario's first clients after the designer opened his own firm in 1963. The apartment, originally built as an artist's studio with 16-foot-high ceilings and expansive windows, was first decorated by George Schreyer, a colleague of Mario's, in blue and white with red accents. The entrance hall of the apartment also doubled as a dining area when Davison entertained. The most dramatic change Mario made was to paint the walls a luscious daffodil yellow. An Indian floral chintz for a club chair and throw pillows relax the room.

OPPOSITE and BELOW *More views of the Davison living room: the goatskin rugs were put in by Schreyer and soon to be changed by Mario for yellow-and-brown-on-white geometric David Hicks-designed rugs.*

More friends, dogs, and chimpanzees ... from left: Honoring Denise Bouché with his chintz crown; the front room of Swifty's restaurant, decorated with Anne Eisenhower in 1999; a chintz-fabric dollar bill that can be laundered—legally; Grace Meigher and Evelyn Lauder; brother Joseph Buatta; Mario receiving an honorary doctorate from Wagner College: "They couldn't give me a degree in interior design, so I asked for it in medicine—gynecology to be exact. It is similar: interior work with women!"; Patricia Altschul in Charleston, SC, with pug Lily; an illustration of the facade of John Fowler's Hunting Lodge; a birthday card of an American bureau bookcase with the caption "Just wanted to get that off my chest," sent to Mario from the Tender Buttons ladies, Diana Epstein and Millicent Safro.

COUNTRY

Hilary and Wilbur Ross
Principal Residence *Palm Beach, Florida*

When Mr. and Mrs. Ross decided to add an entertaining pavilion to their Palm Beach residence, Mario urged the couple to build a large oval ballroom at the structure's front. The result is a pleasing semi-elliptical neoclassical facade fronted with five sets of French doors facing the water. The decorator and the pavilion's architect Thomas Kirchoff won the 2010 Elizabeth L. and John H. Schuler Award from the Preservation Foundation of Palm Beach, recognizing excellence in new construction "in keeping with the character of Palm Beach." The interior's color scheme recalls a seashell, with a pale pink ceiling, a buff and off-white stone floor, and soft white walls. The neutral space puts the dazzling water views—and Mrs. Ross's guests and table decorations—at center stage. When one long table is set up to seat up to forty guests, the two large Schiaparelli sofas are firm enough to offer seating at the table's ends.

PRECEDING SPREAD *Plaster wall lights, designed after a black lacquered Baguès sconce, are mounted on the room's twelve pilasters, with indirect lighting behind. Sets of French doors are mirrored to bring in light and water views.*

OPPOSITE *A round table, layered in purple, red, and pink and surrounded by silver bamboo ballroom chairs, is set for an intimate lunch party.*

ABOVE *The pavilion's powder room is painted off-white with faux-marble decoration and inset with mirrored panels. A silver-leafed Italian mirror and a striped chinoiserie lantern continue the cinematic palette. The vanity is from Nancy Corzine, and the marble floor is inset with roundels.*

258

LEFT *Green hand-painted Gracie Chinese panels cover the walls of this guest bedroom. Scalamandré multicolor striped silk curtains frame the windows and French doors leading out to the terrace and gardens, punctuated by a Lalanne black stone sculpture of a gorilla. The four-poster bone bed is open to the pale pink ceiling.*

BELOW *Blue and white foliate garlands cover the walls of the light-filled master bathroom. His-and-hers mirrored vanities flank the marble tub.*

Biscayne Bay Villa *Florida*

"A House on the Mediterranean" was the design directive for this newly built house on Florida's Biscayne Bay. Together with architect Jeffrey W. Smith, Mario conceived the house as a stately villa that answered the clients' desire for simplicity and serenity. An entrance loggia leads to the living room. The grandness of its proportions with a 25-foot-high barrel-vaulted ceiling and a length of 37 feet are anything but chilly. A warm palette of creams and pinks, deep curvaceous sofas that echo the arches of the architecture, soft carpets from Stark underfoot, and the decorator's particular genius for furniture arrangement make this room as intimate for two as it is for a large gathering.

LEFT *The pickled knotty pine library serves as the sitting room for the two guest rooms on the first floor. Mario notes, "The room is very small and tight, but it is very cozy. The clients play a lot of cards and often sit here by the fire." Throughout the house, a muted tonal palette (here directed by the paneling) is employed for a calming effect.*

BELOW *Mario sits in front of a modern green secretary. "I often use reproductions when it's right. To have found this as a period piece may have been impossible, and the cost wouldn't have made sense."*

263

LEFT *Views of the cerulean sky and water inspired the pale blue-ground mural painted by Robert Jackson. Pictured on the trelliswork panels are the clients' other residences. Mario explains, "You wouldn't want dark wood floors in this room. I had them marbleized in alternating circles and squares to look like a Venetian palazzo." The fantasy of Chippendale-style chairs with silver-leaf legs and mirrored tables is in keeping with the resort setting.*

BELOW *The loggia, which looks out to the water, has a card table for the clients, who are avid bridge players. All the furniture is natural wicker with cushions covered in orange linen with pink piping. The beamed ceiling is painted with Florentine arabesque decoration, continuing the Mediterranean mood. The space is used in all weather, thanks to windows that slide into the floor.*

LEFT *Streamlined Deco-style touches and fanciful curtains in the master bedroom evoke the glamour of a silver-screen siren. Creamy white walls, with a touch of pink for the ceiling, maintain the sumptuous and soothing blancmange palette.*

BELOW *The guest bedroom strikes a tropical note with bamboo furniture and a punchy green and white palm-leaf print from Quadrille.*

Carolands *Hillsborough, California*

This Beaux Arts limestone house, modeled after the French chateau Vaux-le-Vicomte, was built for railroad heiress Harriet Pullman Carolan between 1914 and 1916. The 98-room house was designed by French architect Ernest Sanson, with the 550-acre grounds planned by noted landscape architect Achille Duchêne. Carolan soon ran out of funds and barely inhabited the residence, which was never completed. When Mario's clients purchased it, they literally saved the 65,000-square-foot historic property, now on six acres, from the wrecking ball and soon embarked on a five-year restoration program. The impressive entrance hall, where the architecture takes center stage, is an atrium that spans three stories and is reputed to be the largest interior space in an American private residence. An imperial staircase, covered in a Napoleon III-style carpet from Stark, leads to the *piano nobile* of formal reception rooms. All the working rooms, such as the kitchen, flower room, silver room, and wine cellar, are a few steps down. The decorator explains his approach to the interior: "The house was of its time: drafty and furnished sparely with small-scale chairs. Everything was on legs, and it was all very stiff and formal. We added creature comforts and made it to today's standards."

This sitting room is mainly used for cards and is painted in three shades of blue. The four overdoor oil paintings are original to the house. Mostly French antiques are used throughout in deference to the house's architectural style.

270

ABOVE *The Chinese Room is virtually intact with its original interior. Its name derives from the nineteenth-century Chinese lacquered panels that alternate with vitrines showcasing a collection of Chinese porcelains and artifacts.*

OPPOSITE *In the library the original chandelier set the design directive for the rest of the room. A Napoleon III-style double-sided sofa and fringed lampshades harken to the Gilded Age of the house's first owner.*

273

Tropical Villa *Palm Beach, Florida*

When clients purchased this not-so-old house, Mario applied classical architectural details. "I tried to bring it not up-to-date, but back-to-date," explains the designer. The formal entrance hall has double-height ceilings and measures 25-feet square. A sculptural eighteenth-century Batty Langley–style console table, flanked by a pair of Regency chairs, anchors the space. Above sit two modern Chinese-export-porcelain-style cranes by de Gournay on giltwood brackets. The living room has three arched doorways on opposing walls, with one set leading to the outdoor loggia. The walls were glazed a pale shell pink, and a plush carpet absorbs sound. Brunschwig & Fils Athos chintz was used liberally.

ABOVE *Pocket doors lead into the dining room.*
An arrangement of blanc de chine porcelain
and creamware keeps with the serene tonal palette.

RIGHT *Silvered tea-paper-covered walls, cut crystal,*
and a Venetian mirror add romantic sparkle
in the dining room. A floral-trellis carpet from
Stark connects the room to the outdoors,
and striped curtains play up the room's height.

LEFT *The red lacquered library is off the center hall. Ocelot carpeting and a gold ceiling papered in squares render the room a cozy retreat. "People so often overlook the ceiling—it is the sixth surface in a room and as important as all the others."*

BELOW *To demarcate the family sitting room from the kitchen and breakfast room, it was treated as a tent. A small blue and white print, outlined in ribbon tape, is used for the ceiling canopy.*

FOLLOWING SPREAD *The master bedroom is glazed a blush pink—a color that helps one look their best. Mario advises strongly on choosing a bedroom color that is flattering and enhancing. Striped silk curtains from Tillett pick up the colors in the sky blue-ground floral cretonne from Brunschwig & Fils. Opposite the windows is a painted breakfront dressed with porcelains and books.*

279

LEFT *The master suite's sitting area opens directly on to the loggia adorned with a metal pineapple lantern, bespeaking the house's tropical setting.*

BELOW *Dorothy Draper's iconic rhododendron print is used in the guest bedroom. Mario is completely in accord with her motto, "Decorating is fun!" He remarks, "Decorating is not life or death. I always try to make it fun for clients. If a client does get too serious, I change the subject with a joke."*

Mr. and Mrs. George L. Ohrstrom, Jr. Virginia Residence

The Ohrstroms built this traditional stone and stucco house based on nineteenth-century Piedmont-area precedents. As horse enthusiasts and in anticipation of riding injuries, the couple asked the architect Tommy Beach, Jr. to include an elevator in the plan. In configuring the entrance hall to accommodate this discreetly, Mario suggested the staircase landing incorporate an arched, curtained niche with banquette. "It opens the space and looks like it's continuing to another wing," explains the decorator.

ABOVE *A Colefax and Fowler linen print
is used on the club chairs and fringed curtains.*

RIGHT *The living room's brightness is captured
with cheerful pale lemon yellow glazed walls.
The couple's collection of English horse portraits
is seen throughout. A green eighteenth-century
japanned bureau bookcase sits in the corner.*

ABOVE *The red library is often used for pre- and after-dinner drinks.*
A back-to-back sofa creates the opportunity for a more dynamic furniture
plan, facing the fire on one side and a television on the other. The Regency-
style curtains with attached swagged valance are a favorite of the decorator.

ABOVE *It's all about the details: Mario finishes his club chairs with a decorative tape and contrasting color border at the bottom.*

BELOW *In the blue dining room, green and cream striped curtains and orange Fitzhugh plates on the wall build a striking color scheme.*

Mario is acclaimed for his romantic bedrooms and this one is no exception, landing on the cover of Architectural Digest. The tulip chintz dressing of the bed and windows complements the celery green walls and Buatta-designed carpet. The decorator also designed the Regency-style pyramidal bookcase between the windows.

291

Mr. and Mrs. Arthur Altschul Residence

Centre Island, New York

After years of following Mario's work in magazines, Mrs. Altschul finally had the opportunity to present the decorator with her Buatta file of clippings when she commissioned him to make small updates to the couple's Fifth Avenue residence. When the couple acquired an expansive 1920s country house, they asked the decorator to Buattafy it completely, from floor to pelmet. The thirty-room house was chosen for its spectacular water views and gracious neoclassical architecture. In the living room, lemon yellow-glazed walls provide a luminous backdrop to fine antiques, including a red eighteenth-century japanned bureau bookcase and fantastical shell-form coal scuttle that once belonged to Nancy Lancaster, seen fireside. Maltese-cross broadloom wool carpet, designed by John Fowler, was used on the floor. The client loves collections as much as Mario does. In the staircase hall leading to the guest rooms is a grouping of eighteenth- and nineteenth-century silhouettes.

ABOVE *The stately scale of the living room demands show-stopping curtains. Mario delivered with these confections, topped off with Regency giltwood pelmets draped with checked silk taffeta. One of a pair of sofas flanking the doorway to the library is visible. The curved end is designed to open up the corner.*

RIGHT *"Mario's sense of color is so subtle, refined, and joyous," says Mrs. Altschul. In front of the living room's large picture window overlooking the harbor is a ten-foot-long sofa. Lee Jofa Hollyhock in linen covers the club chairs and throw pillows.*

LEFT *In the dining room a panoramic scenic wallpaper depicting scenes from the American Revolution by Zuber carries indoors the lush garden views that the windows afford. The formality of the eighteenth-century English furniture and crystal chandelier is balanced by the sisal underfoot. The curtains hang from gilded poles and are a multicolored ombré stripe.*

ABOVE *A nineteenth-century gilt metal sunburst clock hung over the sideboard beautifully enhances the scenic wallpaper.*

297

ABOVE *The stunning view of the harbor is framed by curtains made of chinoiserie chintz from Christopher Norman, also used on a sofa and chairs.*

LEFT *Mario glazed the walls a rich red to complement the knotty pine paneling around the chimney breast—a combination he has long admired. A portrait of Pocahontas takes pride of place over the fireplace.*

ABOVE and BELOW *"The blue and white scheme works to cool down a very sunny room,"* notes the decorator. *White-painted mirrors, brackets, and furniture and blue and white Delft continue the color plan.*

LEFT *The master bedroom is swathed in an overscaled periwinkle and white toile from Manuel Canovas. A small-scale settee, copied from a Regency one belonging to Nancy Lancaster at Haseley Court, is placed at the foot of the bed. The row of stuffed gingham cats speaks to the client's love of animals.*

LEFT *This guest bedroom is devoted to dogs, whether in needlework, porcelain, or wool (although felines aren't totally discriminated against here). Lee Jofa's pug chintz is used throughout, relieved by white and off-white polka-dot wallpaper and blue moiré curtains.*

BELOW *The sun porch overlooks the bay. A screen made of green shutters from an old Southern house lends intimacy to the space, and a chenille carpet adds plushness. An antique carved deer trophy found by Mrs. Altschul and the decorator while shopping in France was freshened up with a coat of gray paint.*

Sitting Room *Far Hills, New Jersey*

When it isn't possible to correct a room's architecture, as is the case with this show-house room, shirred fabric hung from wooden poles around the perimeter of the offending walls is an elegant solution. The lemon yellow on the slipper chairs brightens up the forest green cotton walls. The decorator often combines the colors of the outdoors—blue and green. Here a blue and white tree-of-life print covers the sofa and armchair, and a cobalt and Wedgwood blue dhurrie laid on wall-to-wall basketweave sisal is underfoot. Bamboo shades on the bay window bring texture and pattern.

Manor House Master Bedroom

Morristown, New Jersey

This 1976 show-house room displays the decorator's mastery of mixing prints and patterns. Blue denim crisscross-glazed walls enhance the blue and white Pierre Frey zigzag *toile de Nantes* dressing the tester bedstead. The piquant yellow Chinese silk canopy lining injects a thrilling jolt of color. A carved deer trophy mounted between the windows over a black lacquered Portuguese side table reinforces the room's traditional-with-a-twist-of-fantasy style. The pattern on the floor, painted by Michael Murdolo, was inspired by an American quilt.

Connecticut Farmhouse

This 1830 center-hall colonial had been added to over the years, resulting in a rambling floor plan of small rooms. Mario combined three to make the living room. Creamy white-glazed walls and curtains open up the space, while crocus blue grosgrain ribbon used as an outline provides continuity, as does the blue and white floral cotton print Verrieres used throughout. French doors were added to open to the terrace and extensive grounds. "The whole house has the feeling of a garden," says the decorator. The original fireplace wall and mantel were part of the oldest room in the house.

ABOVE *The library was once a screened-in porch. Bright yellow-glazed walls and ample deep seating keep the room cozy year-round. The decorator recalls, "When the husband saw the room for the first time, he immediately asked where the painting of a ship at sea was—I had told his wife that I had hidden it in the staircase closet because it gave me* mal de mer. *I urged him not to hang it over the mantel because the heat of the fire would damage it over time. As soon as the wife and I left the room, we heard a tap, tap, tap. We came back in to see he had just hung an oar, from university days at Yale and signed by all his rowing mates, in the frieze of the mantel. All the pieces were collected over a three-month period, but it looks like they've been there forever. It's what I call the undecorated look."*

310

BELOW *Watermelon pink-glazed walls and a white floor painted with scattered fern fronds brighten the naturally dark dining room. The room's colors all come together in the pink, white, and green curtains at the window.*

Before any decoration was done, the ceiling of the master bedroom was raised to incorporate a Bermuda tray ceiling. The sky blue walls were decorated with trompe-l'oeil trelliswork. "I wanted the feeling of waking up in a gazebo," notes the decorator. "The client loved a pair of George Oakes paintings of flowers I had and asked me to give them to her. I had Robert Jackson copy them on canvas that we glued to the wall, complete with trompe-l'oeil sashes. When she walked into the room and saw them, she exclaimed, 'You are a doll!' But when she realized they were copies, she joked, 'You are a croco-doll!'"

313

Round Living Room *Locust Valley, New York*

The client's exceptional collection of Chinese blue and white porcelain set the direction for this sitting room of stately proportions, originally the house's ballroom. French doors looking out to luxuriant gardens encircle the room, with a fireplace centering one wall and a round white carpet on the floor. Three distinct seating groups positioned around the perimeter of the room make it easy to push the furniture aside and roll up the rug for a dancing party. Apricot walls warm up the crisp blue and white scheme, including a cobalt blue and white linen print on the sofas and chairs. Potted trees take the eye up. Flower-filled vases on eighteenth-century black lacquered stands flank the door to the entrance hall.

Neo-Georgian Library

Morris County, New Jersey

The library was the first room to be completed in a newly built Georgian-style country house in the hills of New Jersey. Oyster white walls and white quilted curtains direct the focus to the blue and white floral Scalamandré linen print that determined the room's color scheme, accented by cherry red. Brass elements, including a Yale Burge tray-top coffee table, were used to warm up the coolness of the blue. "I never want a room to look so rigid that moving a cushion a quarter of an inch ruins the composition," notes the decorator. Books, plants, and a television are all signs of a well lived-in room that the family considered the heart of the house.

And even more friends and dogs ... from left: Jamee Gregory; Mai Hallingby and Mark Gilbertson;
a golden retriever in glasses behind Mario's oversize glasses; wearing the oversize glasses while holding
a dog-topped cane; illustrations of John Fowler's red bedroom and sitting room at the Hunting Lodge.
A Buattatude: Dust is what gives the room a warm, fuzzy feeling.

WEEKEND

Hilary and Wilbur Ross Summer Residence

Southampton, New York

This gracious center-hall colonial once belonged to Millicent Hearst and retains architectural elements from its 1930s Dorothy Draper scheme for the news magnate's wife. Mario first worked on the house in 1976, and in 2000 was asked by the Rosses to give it a major refreshment. The Deco entrance hall with its Draper black and white marble floor and silver tea-paper-covered walls signifies that this isn't a typical summer house. In the living room, biscuit white walls and bleached oak floors are an airy backdrop for the cobalt blue and white cotton print from Brunschwig & Fils used throughout for the seating. Mirrored screens and a Michael Taylor curved-back sofa positioned in the bay window are in keeping with the 1930s mirrored palm-front corner vitrines filled with a collection of seashells, turquoise and pearly glass, and shell plates.

322   ABOVE *Pickled knotty pine paneling designed by architect Charles Muse cozies up the library without making the room skew dark. The herringbone floors were stained in a zigzag Deco manner in espresso, honey, and bone. Brunschwig & Fils La Portugaise, a favorite floral, is used for the curtains and soft upholstery, mixed up with various shades of garden greens and leopard velvet covering the pair of child armchairs.*

ABOVE *Watermelon walls were handpainted by artists Robert Jackson and Haleh Atabeigi to resemble eighteenth-century Chinese wallpaper in the dining room. A pale blue ceiling suggests the sky. The outdoor garden setting is completed with the flowering-treillage carpet, the only floor covering in the main rooms. The fireplace here, as well as the one in the living room, was installed by Dorothy Draper.*

BELOW *French doors in the sunroom lead out to the terrace. Pale lavender walls overlaid with painted trelliswork are decorated with a collection of lettuce-leaf plates by Dodie Thayer. Wicker furniture is covered in a print with lavenders, blues, greens, and pinks.*

LEFT and BELOW *The silver-leaf canopy bed in the master bedroom was designed after Mario's own brown lacquered Regency one from the Brighton Pavilion. The client's love for blue and white is expressed here with a morning glory linen print from Brunschwig & Fils, aqua and white striped papered walls, and a Stark wool carpet. Large windows and French doors look out to the gardens.*

ABOVE *Paneled walls glazed in lime green and
a geometric painted floor enliven this upstairs sitting room.*

RIGHT *A guest room is an exercise in Regency whimsy. The bone
four-poster bed is hung with an orange and cream striped pennant
valance finished with wood tassels and lined in a small blue print.
Zebra sheeting from D. Porthault dresses the bed. A Colefax
and Fowler trellis paper continues the playful exoticism.*

ABOVE *Heavily furnished terraces and porches in wicker and bamboo look out to the Charles J. Stick-designed gardens. During the summer months, the Rosses entertain outdoors in their terrace room under a circular columned portico designed by Stick. The furniture is arranged like a Rorschach test, each side mirroring the other.*

RIGHT *The side porch was redesigned with a fireplace and seating covered in an indoor-outdoor woven zebra fabric reminiscent of the glamorous 1950s nightclub El Morocco.*

LEFT *Architect Charles Muse designed Mario's vision of a Regency pavilion for the pool house, capped off with a triple pagoda roof. In front, pale turquoise Michael Taylor furniture with pale pink cushions was inspired by the set the decorator's Aunt Mary had on her terrace.*

BELOW *The pool house's large center room, which is flanked by changing rooms, is used as a children's playhouse and is painted to resemble a tent, with a blue and lilac awning striped ceiling and trompe-l'oeil boxwood hedges on the wall that continue the line of the outdoor hedge.*

Roxana *On the Sea*

At nearly 160-feet long, *Roxana* is the biggest boat Mario has decorated. The motorboat yacht with six staterooms was custom-built in 1998 by Donald Starkey for longtime clients. For the main living room, the decorator expanded the eight-foot-high ceilings by keeping all surfaces bright with a white ceiling, ivory ocelot carpeting, and creamy walls. A painting slides down to reveal a television. The L-shaped main salon is furnished with three seating areas and a built-in bar. Chintz-covered upholstery infuses the room with the warmth of a floating country house. Just as when he took the transatlantic liner the *Liberté* in 1961 for the Parsons summer program, he wasn't able to enjoy the boat on open waters because of his chronic *mal de mer.*

ABOVE *An octagonal bamboo porch positioned at the front of the yacht is used for card playing and watching television. White wicker covered in a leaf-print chintz furnishes the casual sitting room.*

ABOVE *Mario brings English-country-house style to the seas with floral chintz
and Regency-style curtains. Given the ceiling height, he opted for a very comfortable
king-size sleigh bed over a four-poster in the pale pink master bedroom.
The striped Fortuny curtains emphasize the vertical.*

BELOW *A guest cabin features built-in twin beds and pickled wood paneling
complemented by a Clarence House brown-ground seashell print.*

Mr. and Mrs. George McFadden Residence *Southampton, New York*

Carol and George McFadden sought out the decorator to jazz up their family seaside house. The couple's collection of Asian art and artifacts were important elements in the design. A contemporary approach in the living room was taken with a sparing use of prints and a curated display of *objets*. High-gloss black floors and pale apple green walls lend the room a crisp elegance. A pair of Chinese screens flank the opening to the sunroom.

Mario believes in the importance of first impressions and accordingly glamorized the entrance hall (above), which spans the entire depth of the house and looks out to a lake and extensive gardens by Charles J. Stick. Ivory white and grapefruit-peel-colored walls pop against the floor painted to imitate inlaid marble.

334

LEFT *For a cleaner, modern look in the living room, Mario kept pattern to a minimum, building a color scheme of greens, lilacs, and browns subtly.*

BELOW *The sunroom looks out to spectacular views. The decorator used natural materials in this indoor-outdoor room, including a wicker armchair and seagrass carpeting. A long banquette covered in a white woven cotton is accented by an overscaled ikat from Brunschwig & Fils.*

337

Mr. McFadden found the panoramic Zuber wall panels, The Rape of Jerusalem, at a Chicago auction. Artist Robert Jackson painted the dado as well as above the picture molding to visually extend the antique paper. A mirrored screen, a copy of a Jansen one, masks the doorway into the butler's pantry. Two dining tables with gilt dolphin bases and glass tops are encircled by a set of English box-tufted dining chairs.

LEFT *Mario conceived the library and card room
as a warm evening space that glows by the firelight.
He had the walls and moldings lacquered a deep red,
de-emphasizing the irregular shape of the rooms.
A Billy Baldwin brass and leather card table and caned
Jean-Michel Frank chairs are in the far room.*

BELOW *A French floral cotton print from Braquenié
is used throughout the master bedroom.*

Federal-Style Country House *Litchfield County, Connecticut*

When a couple purchased a 1960s house with no moldings, they commissioned architects Ferguson, Murray & Shamamian to make it over in a 1920s Federal style, and Mario to give it his relaxed English-country-house stamp. The wife's passion for flowers and gardening inspired the design, and many of her arrangements are clustered throughout the house. A note of whimsy in the intimate entryway was struck with black and white prints that were purchased from the Irish Georgian Society, pasted on the walls, and framed with trompe-l'oeil decoration. The adjacent main hall leads to a center staircase "built like a ship's," with an oval fan patera painted on the floor by Robert Jackson to expand the space. The area doubles as a library, with built-in bookshelves holding the couple's collection of red leather-bound books.

LEFT *A center table covered in plaid taffeta divides the large living room and is the perfect place for a large arrangement of the gardens' seasonal offerings. Soft pinks and blues blossom against pineapple yellow walls and curtains. The Aubusson-style carpet, a favorite of the decorator, gives movement to the floor.*

BELOW *A projecting bay window overlooking the gardens offers another opportunity for a seating group with a fitted banquette covered with pillows hand-painted by George Oakes.*

ABOVE *Trompe-l'oeil botanical specimens were painted by Robert Jackson on the paneling of the card room.*

BELOW *Robin's-egg blue Gothic tracery decoration and a faux-marble floor evoke a conservatory setting in the dining room.*

ABOVE *When not set for dinner, the dining table, covered in a Colefax and Fowler chintz,
is dressed with artful arrangements of flowers that Mario's client creates to bring a sampling
of her garden inside. A collection of antique floral creamware is displayed in the niche.*

347

Dark green is splashed throughout the sunroom for a visual transition to the outdoors. The wicker seating and club chair are covered in Elsie de Wolfe's Ferns from Scalamandré.

348

The creamy white-painted master
bedroom puts the focus on the
floral blossoms of the Jean Monro
chintz and the framed prints.
To open up the space, the decorator
used a trellis pattern on the floor—
a favored scheme.

351

Manor House *Southampton, New York*

Mario was asked to rejuvenate this 1960s Norman-style manor house built by the client's grandmother on a 200-acre private family compound. To de-emphasize the immense size of the living room, he created a white box with glazed ivory walls, a white terrazzo floor with white-on-white dhurrie rugs, and ivory curtains at the windows. The decorator chose Matisse colors to warm the space, including the lemon yellow lacquered ceiling and a Chinese-red-ground chintz that immediately draws the eye to the ultra-comfortable, over-upholstered deep armchairs and sofa. A large corner banquette fills the opposite walls.

A blue and white Matisse cotton print from Hinson upholsters the walls, banquette, and folding screen, pulling attention away from the distraction of numerous assymetrically placed French doors and windows. Red-painted chairs with blue and white needlepoint seats inject a burst of color.

355

Historic Barn *New Jersey*

Longtime clients decided to convert an eighteenth-century dairy into a livable dwelling with the help of architect Michael Graves. After Graves was completely finished reimagining the barn, which resulted in a sixteen-room residence, Mario took over. The idiosyncrasies of the historic structure, like the old wood-beamed ceiling, were respected while accommodating all the modern creature comforts. An unusual nineteenth-century table with horselike carved legs greets visitors in the entrance hall. A stone floor and potted trees connect this space to the outdoors. To enter the main living room, one descends a staircase. Mario lets the architectural bones take center stage through a restrained color palette, spare use of pattern, and an astute placement of furniture. Antiques are simple and were chosen for their form. The iron chandeliers were designed by Graves and reference wagon wheels.

356

OPPOSITE *A Graves-designed double-sided stone fireplace divides the living room from the dining room. An antique weathervane of a lion, the client's favorite animal, presides over the mantel. Mario employed a double sofa to create intimately scaled seating groups.*

BELOW *Though not completely enclosed, the dining room's focus on the fireplace and the round table creates an intimate setting.*

OPPOSITE and ABOVE *An overscaled pomegranate toile*
in magenta on ivory from Manuel Canovas is used
throughout the guest bedroom. Rustic antiques,
all acquired specifically for the project, are appropriate
for this relaxed country setting, says Mario.

361

Nancy and Frank S. Benson, Jr. Residence *Delray Beach, Florida*

The Bensons' collection of antiques and paintings set the elegant tone for the decoration of their wintertime apartment. "I wanted the rooms to capture the feeling of a Prendergast. In this hot climate, I thought every room should look especially light and cool," explains Mario. A color-field painting by Robert Natkin hangs over the sofa in the pale lilac living room. Comfort goes beyond deep upholstery—all the seating has tables and lamps handily nearby.

363

ABOVE *Mario placed a corner sofa at an angle to open up the living room and provide an opportunity for another seating group.*

OPPOSITE *The sunroom opens out to an extensive terrace. The walls are bleached cypress. The same floral chintz, Athos, that is used in the living room covers the sofa to create a visual flow.*

365

The rhododendron green library is lacquered to reflect the natural light. The designer enclosed the terrace with glass walls to form an alcove for the card table.

367

ABOVE *Pale floors throughout the apartment help keep
the rooms bright and airy. In the dining room, the wood floors
are painted in faux marble.*

RIGHT *The master bedroom's walls are striéed in peachy pink.
Mario masterfully mixed pink and white florals, stripes,
ribbon, and trellis prints.*

368

Neo-Georgian House

Bedford, New York

After years of living in a chrome and glass apartment, Mario's clients craved color for their traditional house outside the city. For the large living room, spinach green crisscross-glazed and lacquered walls provide a backdrop for bursts of lemon, raspberry, sky blue, and lime green to pop against. "This isn't just a *living* room. It's a *live* room that feels dramatic and radiates warmth and welcome." Three seating groups allow for the room to be as comfortable for two as it is for eighteen.

"The bedroom has the charm of a Georgian boudoir,"
notes Mario. A lavender and white printed vinyl covers the walls,
and painted fern fronds appear to be scattered on the white floor.
Swiss tambour panels are hung to form the tester bed, "a room within a room."

373

Carriage House *New Jersey*

A couple's country retreat, a carriage house that was once used as a garage, was bathed in the wife's preferred jelly bean brights of lime, grape, and strawberry. The blue and white trellis wallpapered entry is "like stepping into the sky," says Mario. A sliver of the red-painted floor is visible under the straw matting in the entrance hallway. In the lime green-sponged living room, country antiques suit the house's informality.

ABOVE and RIGHT *Using the same wall color and floor covering throughout the main living space makes the open floor plan feel even more expansive. Rainbow striped curtains and a quilt-covered table festively combine all the colors.*

Park Avenue Apartment

New York, New York

The owners specifically asked for a gardenlike setting for their city residence. Accordingly, the living room and dining room walls were painted a pineapple yellow to capture the sun, which was complemented by Braquenié's Le Grand Arbre chintz and large sky blue French linen dhurrie carpet in the living room. In later years, when the client thought the curtains looked tired and faded, Mario suggested glazing the walls a deep foliage green in a crisscross strié to crisp the white of the chintz. Bursts of poison green add energy to the scheme, and white-painted furniture, instead of dark brown wood, keeps it airy and bright. A sofa placed in the corner opens up the room and creates another seating group. In the summertime, the curtains and rug are slipcovered in off-white canvas with brass edged corners.

ABOVE *The living room opens on to the dining room, which retained its pineapple yellow walls. The decorator notes, "The living room chintz is deliberately repeated in the table's daytime cover, a nice echo, and the French chairs were given an outdoor summertime air with cane backs and basketweave seat coverings." White linen curtains trimmed in blue ribbon hang at the window.*

RIGHT *The eighteenth-century portrait over the fireplace prompted the red, white, and blue scheme in the library. "This is a room for lovers of red. The blue carpet is a perfect foil for the red—and so is the blue of the slipcover fabric, an African batik cotton print."*

380

The master bedroom was transformed into a verdant bower with
a Brunschwig lemon-and-leaves chintz on the walls and at the windows.
The rosemary lattice painted on the floor by artist Robert Jackson
gives the long room a wider dimension. The David Hicks-style
tester bed is hung in white linen with aqua grosgrain trim.

383

*Of wigs and beards ... counterclockwise from upper left: Mario donning a chintz "no-smoking" jacket made by Joan Kron and hairpiece
to celebrate the launch of his first collection of floral fabrics; bewigged with Judy Green; life of the party Jackie Weld-Drake;
bearded at the wedding of Jack and Dolly Geary with mother-in-law Hilary Geary Ross looking on; Christopher Spitzmiller (right),
lampmaker extraordinaire, with Sam Allen; a humorous card "The Soprano Family, Redecorated" featuring Mario;
at a dinner party, the Prince of Chintz lets his hair down with the help of a female guest's head of hair.
A Buattatude: Your husband called. He said you can buy anything you want!*

FROM

MARIO

rio,
t feen I had
! I have not

SOPRA

MARIO BUATTA
THE MAKING OF AN AMERICAN MASTER

BY EMILY EVANS EERDMANS

IT HAS BEEN SAID that Mario Buatta is a household name in some extraordinary households. While this is true, it is the imprint he has made on popular culture—as clearly evidenced by his inspiration of a *Jeopardy!* game show question—that is even more remarkable. Before the Internet, before the deluge of how-to television, Mario was one of a handful of interior decorators in the twentieth century to attain widespread celebrity in his own time. Though his catchy The Prince of Chintz moniker aided and abetted his renown, it is his romantic vision and genius for creating visual and sensual comfort that have claimed a devout following ever since he opened his doors in 1963. Mario is touted for bringing the English-country-house style to America, but the generosity and exuberance of his work reflect a sunny optimism that is wholly American.

The landscape in which Mario came of age was the white-glove, tasteful decorating of such firms as Mrs. Henry Parish II, McMillen, and Elisabeth Draper, where he worked for a four-month stint in 1962. Clients, both establishment and the newly arrived, sought vaguely Louis or Georgian formal settings that were typically blandly colored in pale yellows and apricots and contained good antiques, paintings, and porcelains. There was nothing particularly personal or expressive about these rooms and it was precisely to achieve this acceptable *comme il faut* look that clients used these designers.

Mario's exuberant Aunt Mary and the unconventional interior decorator Rose Cumming were major early influences on him. Both expressed their potent personalities through style, resulting in highly individual interiors. When faced with Draper's conventional good taste, it can be no surprise that Mario reacted with indifference. While her firm boasted some of the country's most elite families as clients, this was not enough to seduce Mario into the received style. On-the-job learning was more the rule than not for most aspiring designers at the time, even fifty years after the interior decoration department was established by Frank Alvah Parsons at the New York School of Art (later renamed Parsons School of Design and now Parsons The New School for Design). A few firms, such as McMillen, required their designers to have degrees in design, but most learned the profession while employed, and it was highly desirable to get experience at a larger firm where one could learn the brass tacks of decorating as well as best business practices, the psychology of handling clients, and the names in a fiercely guarded Rolodex of sources.

A letter to Mario
from one of his first clients:

Start here at your own risk. Darling…darling… darling… How could I be so lucky as to have YOU needless to say I can't live without those mah-velous vases. AND I do want that chandelier in soft moss green but no—no shades on it. Advise [sic] on console message did not come thru clear. The easel is to display current works of art by you + me of course don't be so modest dear boy. House and Garden *ought to know about you to say nothing of* Connoisseur *but then of course what of these earthly pleasures when a word of praise from A. Hudes is what we really crave… I looked and looked in vain thinking one of those little angels on Halloween must be my MARIO but alas no. What about Paris this year love or would Morocco be more your cup of tea. AND so forget Rose Cummings [sic] and think only of me. Yours always Madame Butterfly.*

Mario soon left Draper. He was approached by a design colleague, George Schreyer, who was now associated with the firm Irvine and Fleming. Schreyer hailed from an old family in Princeton, New Jersey, and had established his own roster of clients culled from friends and family. He was highly social and kept a schedule of late hours on the town. He urged Mario to interview with the firm, and in 1962 Mario began working as Keith Irvine's assistant. Irvine, who previously worked for John Fowler and Mrs. Parish, infused his rooms with country-house details and the same spirit of individuality that had so enthralled Mario when he first saw pictures of Nancy Lancaster's famous yellow drawing room. Under Keith's tutelage, he learned more about achieving this style.

George Schreyer provided Mario with one of the most important opportunities of his career—sadly as a result of his untimely death in 1963. In May of that year, Mario opened his own firm with a raft of Schreyer's uncompleted projects on deck, including the New Jersey house of his mother, Polly, who was a terrific Mario advocate. One of these included the Upper East Side apartment of Gates Davison, a scion of an illustrious Long Island Gold Coast family. The apartment was originally built as an artist's studio, and the living room featured a double-height ceiling with outsized windows streaming in natural light. Mario kept much of what Schreyer had installed but introduced a new coloration of lemon yellow walls and curtains, and

Indian chintz. Mario also decorated Davison's offices for the New York World's Fair, where he was chief of protocol. Another early client was Gloria Schiff, one of the famously fashionable O'Connor twins. After spying Mario's apartment through the window while walking by, she dropped her card in his mailbox. In 1968 he decorated her Park Avenue apartment, which he continued to refresh over the next decade.

Mario steadily grew his practice with referrals. From the very beginning, he forged close friendships with his clients and worked with several members and generations of one family. On one overnight stay with Princeton clients, he earned the nickname Uncle Lush because he was caught foraging in the kitchen at nighttime. Though his clients assumed he was looking for a tipple, he was actually searching for a snack to supplement the restrained dinner portion served.

Actress Elaine Stritch was another early client. She wanted to live inside an egg and requested that Mario soak her West 57th Street apartment living room in a zingy yellow, including all the woodwork, ceilings, and doors. She requested the same all-over treatment in her bedroom and bathroom, which was covered in a cotton print of forget-me-nots and yellow butterflies. When she ordered an extra five yards to make a peignoir, Mario exclaimed that her husband would never find her. "That's the point!" she riposted.

For a client's card room, previously decorated by Billy Baldwin in beige,
Mario advocated a rich chocolate brown lacquer to make it cozy and enveloping.

Mario showing Rudolf Bing, right, a bargello sample for an office chair during the decoration of the offices of the Metropolitan Opera.

METROPOLITAN OPERA

THE GENERAL MANAGER

August 3, 1966

Mr. Mario Buatta
115 East 72 Street
New York City

Dear Mr. Buatta:

I just meant to write you a note to say how beautiful I think the room has come out when your lovely flowers arrived for which I now have to add my thanks.

I really think it is all very nice, and I am grateful. Kind regards.

Yours sincerely,

Rudolf Bing

RB:dd

In 1966 his reputation was sufficiently established to win the commission to help decorate the new Metropolitan Opera House at Lincoln Center alongside such big names as Billy Baldwin and Angelo Donghia. Mario adopted a contemporary black and white scheme punctuated with splashes of citron for the executive lobby and offices. White-on-white striped Fiberglas window treatments were complemented by a graphic geometric black and white carpet. Deep gauffraged velvet banquettes of cadmium yellow and potted trees added punch and softness to the setting.

As the sixties unfurled and unraveled, from pillbox hats to bell-bottoms, a new guard was dominating the covers of shelter magazines. Mario cites the team of Edward Zajac and Richard Callahan—known for their bold patterns on patterns—as two of the most featured talents of this time. He once tried his hand at this eclectic style for a magazine story, but after a prospective client canceled her appointment upon seeing it, he made a decision not to diverge from his Anglophilic tastes. Not everyone understood or appreciated Mario's look. In 1963, after Mario related his admiration for John Fowler's decoration style in comparison to Billy Baldwin's, Zajac, who had trained under Baldwin,

Mario designed this room for House & Garden's *April 1973 feature "Decorate-It-Yourself with Sheets."*
Anemone- and check-printed sheets are mixed with signature Buatta aplomb.

witheringly rejoined: "Billy Baldwin has more talent in one finger than you'll ever have in your two hands." However, Mario always knew he would realize success.

From the outset, Mario sought out public ways to show off his work and attract more notice and clients. One of the first show houses he participated in was in 1969 in Greenwich, Connecticut. For this room he did lemon peel-glazed walls set off by a coral-painted canopy bed (see page 32). This room launched Mario dually—on a national level and in another social sphere. After the room appeared, in the September 1969 issue of *House & Garden*, Mitzi Newhouse, the glamorous wife of Condé Nast owner Samuel I. Newhouse and a regular on the International Best-Dressed list, picked up the phone and hired him to replicate it for her. As her son Donald remembers, she had very strong ideas about what she liked and wanted. The result was very close to the original, with the same yellow-pink coloration, but with slight modifications.

Afterwards, Mario appeared regularly in the pages of *House & Garden* and *House Beautiful*. From contributing small blurbs on how to slipcover with sheets and fashioning backdrops for stories such as "Parties from the Freezer," he quickly graduated to feature articles. Mario's fresh, pretty look anticipated the profusion of prints that swept the pages of the magazines and found their way into the lines of mainstream manufacturers. *House & Garden* editor-in-chief Mary Jane Pool notes that for the first time affordable, stylish printed sheets came on the market that were previously only purveyed by such high-priced marques as D. Porthault. Magazines ran copious sheets stories, on how to dress canopy beds and upholster walls with them, and Mario gamely styled several of them.

Though Mario never hired his own publicity person, he was a natural showman and always made time to give magazines a pithy quotation or whip up a setting for one of their trend stories. Diantha Nype, who was the director of publicity for the Kips Bay Decorator Show House for many years as well as the namesake for one of Mario's fabrics, noted, "Mario has done what other designers have been unable to do or ... have chosen not to do. And that is to use the media, as it is there to be used."

With the help of florist Ronaldo Maia, Mario transformed a client's dining room into a woodland whimsy for a 1970 luncheon party.

OPPOSITE *Mario cut the chintz ribbon to unveil the street sign for Designers Way outside New York's Decoration & Design Building. D&D owner Charles Cohen, left, holds Mario's ladder steady.*

ABOVE and OPPOSITE *Two views of Mario's second show-house room, which was featured on the cover of the* New York Times' The Home *magazine on October 1, 1972. It featured spinach green crisscross-glazed walls, and squishy sofas and chairs in a blue-and-green-on-white-ground tobacco-leaf print. An ivory Fowleresque decorative taffeta sash supports a horse painting. The day after its publication, Angelo Donghia offered Buatta a job, but Mario was already established on his own and respectfully declined.*

In 1971, *Collier's Yearbook* illustrated Mario's sitting room and hailed a return to tradition. His densely layered rooms splashed with saturated colors and boldly patterned chintzes were considered idiosyncratic and even eccentric when he first came on the scene. The prevailing modernism of the sixties favored a more spare aesthetic, but by the end of the seventies, the pendulum of fashion had swung toward traditionalism and Mario.

The May/June 1974 issue of *Architectural Digest* was Mario's first feature in the magazine and marked the beginning of an important relationship between him and the magazine. It was helmed by Paige Rense, officially made editor-in-chief the following year, who was pivotal in transforming the magazine from what began in 1920 as a trade directory into the premiere shelter magazine showcasing how the very rich and very famous lived. Her recipe of Hollywood celebrity and the international jet set soon culled enviable newsstand sales and a huge following, from Midwest housewives to Park Avenue matrons. As one person commented, it was the only place you ever saw a Rolls-Royce advertisement. One of Rense's first tactics was to approach leading designers and form a relationship through which the magazine supported the designer by publishing his or her work and in turn the designer gave her first refusal. Over time, as the power and influence of the magazine grew, this expanded to total exclusivity and loyalty to the magazine. It was well worth the exchange. Many of the designers and architects could be assured of more than one new job after appearing in its pages—a record the other shelter magazines couldn't come close to matching.

With his lack of pretensions and stock of practical jokes, he charmed his way as a sought-after dinner guest and appeared regularly in society columns such as *Suzy* (the byline of client Aileen Mehle) and Julie Baumgold's *Mr. Peepers*. Baumgold recounted in "Far Out in Far Hills" one of Mario's lectures to a garden club. Employing his comedic skills, he began the talk in typical fashion—with jokes. He introduced a prop book, *Bringing the Outdoors In*, which promptly opened to a cascade of dead leaves, dried flowers, and rubber snakes. As early as 1965, Mario was making a

May 2, 1967

Mr. Mario Buatta
115 East 72nd Street
New York, New York

Dear Mario:

Knowing you're an artist first and a businessman second, you will undoubtedly forget to ask for a letter of recommendation upon completion of our apartment in the Ritz Tower, so Rita and I will send you one anyway.

You have done a truly outstanding job in merging our two very different tastes, both of which are also different from your own. The coordinating of the hundreds of minor and major details, which was required in this project, was superbly handled by you in completing the apartment on schedule.

You have our combined thanks and our best wishes for a rapid rise in your chosen field.

splash on the social scene, even appearing in a *Glamour* magazine article on young with-it Manhattanites. In 1974 columnist Enid Nemy included him on her *New York Times'* "Most-Wanted List" of the city's extra men, which also included Bill Blass and Jerry Zipkin. Mario's extroverted personality was a key instrument in growing his business. He was perhaps the most famous decorator in America by the time playwright Jay Presson Allen inserted him into *Tru*, her play about Truman Capote that debuted in 1989. In one scene, Capote laments, about the fallout from *Answered Prayers*, "No billionaire ever got bit by Mario Buatta."

In 1977 a museum dedicated to the Duchess of Windsor was being planned at her grammar school, Oldfields, in Glencoe, Maryland. The duchess was the honorary chairperson, and Diana Vreeland—who as special consultant of the Metropolitan Museum's Costume Institute had secured permission for the duchess's blue Mainbocher wedding dress to be copied—was among those on the advisory committee, along with CZ Guest and Madame Gerald van der Kemp, the wife of Versailles's head curator. Mario was put in charge with co-chair Louis Guariglia, Saks Fifth Avenue's design director, of overseeing the interiors, including a replication of the Windsors' library in their villa outside the Bois de Bologne. Although the museum was never realized, his involvement with the initial stages indicates he had achieved a certain social stature and celebrity.

ABOVE *A rare photograph documenting Peggy Lee and her (surprise) evening with Zip the Chimp at The Ballroom.*

TOP LEFT *A letter from Mr. and Mrs. Frederick B. Ayer (Rita Delafield Kip), two of Mario's earliest clients.*

Mario with Lynn Johnson, photographed for the November 1965 issue of Glamour.

The restaurant Mortimer's, owned by Glenn Birnbaum (looming above), was a New York institution for the social set. Mario remembers leaving Mortimer's one day and offering beauty magnate Estée Lauder a ride. He recalls: "I said, 'Here's my car—it's the yellow one with a checkerboard and a light.' In the car I told her that I remembered when she opened her first counter at B. Altman's. The taxi driver overheard us and said he always bought his wife Youth Dew. Estée said, 'Tell her you had Estée Lauder in your back seat.' He replied, 'When you get home, tell your husband Cary Grant was your driver.'" Philip James Herman's illustration references Mario's boxing match with Zip the Chimp on Malcolm Forbes's yacht with Billy Norwich, Forbes, and Joan Rivers also at the table.

Dina Merrill and Ted Hartley hosted a star-studded dinner for eighteen, won by Marvin and Lee Traub to benefit City Mission. Dr. Ruth Westheimer played the hostess, Joan Rivers acted as the waitress, and Mario served as the butler. Other attendees included Grace Mirabella, Iris Love, and restaurateur George Lang.

Not like Mama's
Ivana Trump reacts to Mario Buatta's rubber chicken during a celebrity cook-in to benefit the March of Dimes in New York Tuesday. The cook-in, featuring celebrities such as interior designer Buatta and Mike Tyson, was held at the Plaza Hotel, which is owned by Trump's husband Donald.

Associated Press

"I found that the crazier I behave, the more people like it."
— MARIO BUATTA

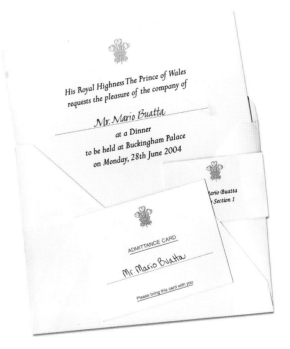

His Royal Highness The Prince of Wales
requests the pleasure of the company of

Mr. Mario Buatta

at a Dinner
to be held at Buckingham Palace
on Monday, 28th June 2004

ADMITTANCE CARD

Mr. Mario Buatta

Please bring this card with you

TOP RIGHT *Cooking with Ivana Trump, November 1989.*

BOTTOM RIGHT *An invitation to a dinner at Buckingham Palace, which Mario attended with his plastic pet cockroach, Harold, who was a big hit with Prince Charles.*

399

Artist Sander Witlin captures a party given in honor of society bandleader Peter Duchin and attended by luminaries Lena Horne, Jacqueline Onassis, Pamela and Averell Harriman, Kitty Carlisle Hart, and a Truman Capote look-alike, among others. Mario is illustrated sitting on a sofa with Nan Kempner.

ABOVE LEFT *Clement Conger, White House curator, and Nancy Kissinger look on at a pagoda-form cake celebrating Mario's fifteen years as chairman of the Winter Antiques Show.*

ABOVE RIGHT *Mario created an entire environment around a table setting for Tiffany, incorporating dining chairs from his John Widdicomb collection.*

In an interview with Mario Amaya for *Interview* magazine, Mario credited the insult comic Pudgy with teaching him the advantages of disarming what might be an intimidating audience with insults laced with honey. "I found that the crazier I behave, the more people like it. I insult people because I want to be liked." As one person on the scene commented, otherwise buttoned-up or frosty personages like Sister Parish could only laugh when presented with a fright-wig-wearing Mario or his plastic pet cockroach, Harold. "Otherwise it would be obvious they were a stick in the mud," observes a colleague. Mario, who appreciated the importance of having one's name in the papers, treated his extracurricular socializing as an extension of his business. One of his most elaborate jokes that made the news was taking Zip the Chimp to see the chanteuse Peggy Lee perform at The Ballroom, after receiving encouragement from Lee's assistant, Bernard Lafferty (who would famously inherit a slice of Doris Duke's fortune). Zip applauded and blew kisses at the end of each number, until Lee finally said, "Perhaps it's someone's bedtime." After the show, she allowed her photo to be taken with the chimpanzee, but withheld permission for it to be printed in the next morning's paper.

A prestigious jewel in Mario's social crown was bestowed when he was asked in 1973 to chair the Winter Antiques Show, New York's foremost annual antiques show, held at the Park Avenue Armory. After successfully chairing the silent auction of Les Boutiques de Noël, a charity Christmas bazaar run by elegant Upper East Side ladies, Mario was approached by Louis W. Bowen to oversee the show's loan exhibition of selections from the Metropolitan Museum of Art. He created a fifteen-foot-wide pavilion to showcase the furniture and paintings on display. After netting a meager $30,000 profit for the benefiting charity, East Side Settlement House, the show needed to make a change or close. Mario remembers, "Opening night they'd get 600 or 700 people. You could shoot a cannon down the aisles by eight o'clock. It was mainly country dealers—one was even handing out baked goods they had brought in." Mario was asked to step in as chairman and invigorate what had become a frowsy matron. He took the role seriously and ushered in a new era by making the opening night a major social event and bringing fresh blood to the show. International dealers were invited for the first time to exhibit—to the consternation of the current exhibitors and the old guard who faithfully upheld the traditions of the show.

Mario fashioned a cobwebbed table setting, inspired by Miss Havisham and her wedding night that never happened, for a benefit evening at the New York Public Library.

However, it was Mario's brainchild, with the assistance of publicist Joanne Creveling, to inject the celebrity quotient as well as to embrace the Nouvelle Society that was exploding in the seventies and eighties with money to burn and, most important, to spend on tickets and antiques. Mario credits Creveling with mining fashion circles to bring glamour—and more press attention—to the show. The turning point came in 1977, when Mario invited Lee Radziwill to decorate the Armory's historic Tiffany Room, which she festooned with lime green taffeta moiré and amaryllis arrangements by florist Jean-Jacques Bloos. Mario recalls, "It was only a one-night room, but every day of the show people poured in looking for the Lee Radziwill room." Opening-night numbers exploded from 800 to 2,800. In years following, prominent fashion designers, including Bill Blass, Ralph Lauren, Carolina Herrera, and Oscar de la Renta, continued the tradition of decorating the Tiffany Room. That same year Mario partnered with Clem Conger, curator of the White House Diplomatic Reception Rooms, to select fine furniture and paintings from the State Department for the show's loan exhibition. Conger and Mario would work together again on the restoration of Blair House almost a decade later. In 1990, after over fifteen years as chair and bringing annual profits close to the million-dollar mark, a personal goal of his, Mario decided to step down.

Over the years Mario has participated in dozens of decorator show houses. His show-house philosophy of veering on the side of over-embellishment resulted in one of his most famous rooms, if not *the* most, to date. For the 1984 Kips Bay Boys Club Decorator Show House, located in a neo-Federal red brick townhouse at 36 East 74th Street, previously the home of the George Whitneys and Dorothy Paley, Mario created a lavender-striéed striped bedroom offset by the cobalt blue and white chintz Verrieres. Presiding over the room was a bed magnificently tented with shirred handkerchief linen. Mark Hampton's observation—"Mario has a storybook kind of look, a picturesque quality"—unequivocally applied to this room.

Mario's 1984 Kips Bay show-house room continues to garner sighs and accolades,
including the cover of and an unprecedented seven pages in House Beautiful.
Artist Jeremiah Goodman says that he saw the room a thousand times and had to paint it.

Dear Mario –

Thank you so very much for all the trouble you went to to send me Nancy Lancaster's address – on all those lovely postcards – "Green Animals" Topiary Gardens was my favorite place – We used to go there as children and have fresh tomato juice from the garden in wine glasses, from tiny old indomitable Miss Brayton who owned it – I will save the postcard forever because I never had one –

I hope that Lee's birthday will be annually celebrated – and that you will have the same sartorial experience every year – because it was so delightful to sit with you for a long time – Every lovely thing Lee has told me about you is true –

gratefully Jackie

Reporter Chauncey Howell covered the show house for NBC's *Live at Five* local news and dubbed Mario "The Prince of Chintz." The rhyming nickname stuck and was even encouraged by Mario, who in jest could be seen wearing everything from a suit to a cowboy hat made of the glazed printed cotton. While he naturally gravitated to incorporating chintz in his interiors, he also understood the value of having a trademark. "It's good to be known for something," he has cannily said. As *Spy* magazine pointed out in its October 1989 article lampooning the design and decorating industry, clients choose designers precisely for the signature look they are associated with, and with his new royal title, the Mario Buatta look was even more easily understood and consumed by potential clients.

PLAYBILL

ST. JAMES THEATRE

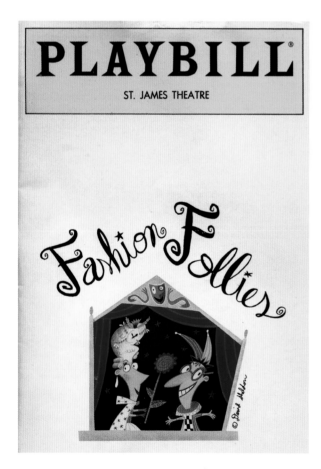

Fashion Follies

406

CLOCKWISE FROM TOP *A letter from Jacqueline Onassis; Mario tipped a chintz cowboy hat at a benefit party hosted by Texan Liz Smith; the set of Wendy Wasserstein's play* The Sisters Rosensweig, *debuting in 1992, incorporated Mario's chintzes. Wasserstein and Mario struck up a friendship, and she later asked him for decorating advice. When he surveyed her collection of dolls, stuffed animals, and what she herself described as "a cross between a Smith College date parlor and the novelty section of the local import store," he teasingly replied, "Take a match to it!"; In 1992 Mario was asked to participate in* Fashion Follies, *a Broadway revue in honor of Leo Lerman, the hallowed Condé Nast editor. Lily Tomlin, Gregory Hines, and Betty Comden were a few who took the stage. Critic John Heilpern from the* New York Observer *hailed Mario as "an unexpected virtuoso star." He appeared with Anne Francine and canine-couture chintz-dressed dogs running through a hoop. He then addressed the audience, saying that it was difficult to see, as he was wearing Ralph Lauren contact lenses that allowed him to see only polo ponies running through the audience.*

Mario gamely embraced The Prince of Chintz moniker and donned a suit made in one of his own floral prints for the July 1986 cover of Manhattan,inc.

Henry Ford II

March 13,
1981

Mr. Mario Buatta,
New York, N. Y. 10021

Dear Mario:

Now that we have moved into 160 and
the house is 99% complete, I wanted to
write and tell you what a marvelous job
you did in decorating it for us. Kathy
and I are terribly pleased with the total
house, and feel that it is a happy, warm
and beautiful place in which to live,
thanks to your efforts to accomplish same.

Congratulations on a job well done!

Best Regards
Harry

HFII:jc

ABOVE *Malcolm Forbes's living room in New Jersey hunt country.*

TOP LEFT *Mario designed a dollar bill in honor of client
Mariah Carey for* Money *magazine.*

MIDDLE and BOTTOM LEFT *Notes from appreciative
and famous clients Henry Ford II and journalist
Barbara Walters.*

BARBARA WALTERS

Mario dear —
Once more —
thank you for remembering
with that wonderful silver
postcard. So thoughtful
and loving of you.
A big hug
Barb

While bold-faced names such as Malcolm Forbes, both Henry Ford II and his daughter Charlotte, Henry Kissinger, and Barbara Walters regularly sought out Mario's services, one of his plummiest jobs was the restoration of Blair House, the White House's guest quarters in Washington, D.C. where visiting heads of state are hosted. A gas leak and errant chandelier in 1982 prompted a restoration program that included a new decoration scheme by Mario and Mark Hampton. Blair House had grown to incorporate four houses joined together—Blair House and Blair-Lee House on Pennsylvania Avenue and two others on Jackson Avenue. The designers divvied up the 112 rooms by each taking two houses and only meeting in the hallway—with the mandate to make everything flow. The three-year, $13 million project was completed in 1988.

The House Buatta-ful

Mario recollects first meeting fashion mogul-to-be Ralph Lauren in the late 1960s, when Lauren was selling his extra-wide ties to Bloomingdale's. He once gave the designer a lift to New Hope, Pennsylvania, in his new bottle green Jaguar during the full heat of the summer. A failed electrical system meant no air conditioning and the immovable windows sealed tight, prompting Lauren to beg off for the return leg. It is interesting to contemplate if either of these native New Yorkers, who would both become household names by interpreting aristocratic English style for a democratic American audience, realized at that time how much in common they had.

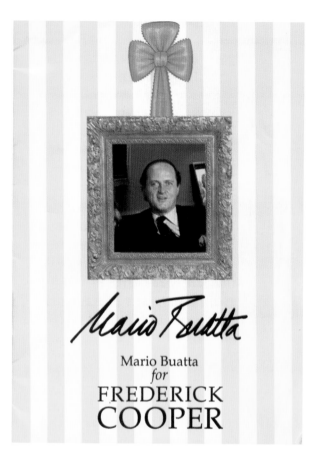

Mario Buatta
for
FREDERICK
COOPER

Mario wasn't the first interior decorator to license his name. In the 1970s Angelo Donghia had already put his name on everything from dinnerware to bed linens, and there were others, like T. H. Robsjohn-Gibbings, who designed furniture for the Grand Rapids furniture company John Widdicomb in the 1940s. However, with a particular flair for self-promotion, Mario's products achieved especially high visibility and were up front and center during the eighties. His mentor from Parsons summer school, Stanley Barrows, extolled, "Mario has made it possible for a wide segment of the American consumer world to enjoy and possess household furnishings of a type until now restricted to the super rich. He has promoted the spread of good taste in every part of the country."

MARIO BUATTA
FOR
JOHN WIDDICOMB COMPANY®

CLOCKWISE FROM TOP *Sales brochures for Mario's collection of lamps for Frederick Cooper and furniture for John Widdicomb; Mario's Aromatique home fragrances.*

RIGHT *A department store setting showing off Diantha, the most popular print from Mario's first collection of sheets for Revman, which met with great success.*

"Mario has made it possible for a wide segment of the American consumer world to enjoy and possess household furnishings of a type until now restricted to the super rich."
— STANLEY BARROWS

ABOVE *A Chippendale-inspired tray table from Mario's John Widdicomb line.*

LEFT *Mario pulls one of his lamps for Frederick Cooper with a tie.*

Mario stands in one space of a five-room model house he designed in 1988 for B. Altman's seventh floor.
The display was such a success that the department store devoted six windows on Fifth Avenue to it for a month.

ABOVE LEFT *Winterthur, Henry Francis du Pont's historical-house museum in Wilmington, Delaware, dedicated to American decorative arts, asked Mario to decorate the first floor of the house with their new line of reproduction fabrics, wallcoverings, and furniture.*

ABOVE RIGHT and OPPOSITE *In 1982* House & Garden *paid tribute to Winterthur by asking Mario to style, in a modern way, a New York brownstone living room with the museum's various lines of reproductions. A room that looks lived-in and full of personality is achieved with attention to every detail, from the latest magazines to a ready supply of firewood.*

In 1984 Mario signed on as spokesman for the Krone-a-Phone Compact 1000 telephone, "available in a unique palette of colors selected by trendsetting decorator Mario Buatta." Mario's first foray into licensing was the following year with a line of five fabrics in twenty-two different colorways manufactured by Fabriyaz, available to the trade and retailing in department stores for $33 a yard. He was soon approached by Federated Department Stores, which put his own boutiques in their stores across the country, including several upscale department stores. Potpourris in Honeysuckle and Holiday Forest by Aromatique were next and went into all of his rooms at Blair House. In 1988 he launched a collection of six bed-linen lines for Revman, a division of Laura Ashley, which included bedding, balloon shades, tablecloth rounds, and decorative pillows, and, pre-dating thread-count mania, were a blend of 60 percent cotton and 40 percent polyester. His beginnings at Bonwit Teller and B. Altman & Co. gave him an appreciation for the importance of alluring product display, and he showed off the sheets with panache in a model room at Macy's Corner Shop Antiques Galleries. The same year he unveiled his nineteen-piece line of furniture for John Widdicomb, which was based on Mario-selected antique pieces, many in the Regency style and featuring painted and lacquered finishes. In the 1990s, a dozen different lines—fabrics with Waverly and Schumacher, lamps by Frederick Cooper, carpets, needlepoint, and a collection of framed pictures and mirrors—all diffused the Buatta name across the country.

Mario's weekly diary of appointments and to-do lists.

Given Mario's annual workload of seventy ongoing jobs, an expanding portfolio of licenses, and a relentless social schedule, it astonishes many to find out that the designer has had few assistants over the past several years. Clients have joked that Mario went through assistants like paper towels, and he himself has acknowledged that he is a demanding and extremely particular employer. An *Architectural Digest* article on fashion designer Cathy Hardwick's apartment noted that her young assistant Tom Ford was found hiding from Mario's directives during the photo shoot.

Betty Barrett was Mario's longest-lasting assistant and worked for the designer between 1968 and 1978. During the time his office was still based in his apartment, Betty was corralled into Mario's bedroom walk-in closet to contain her smoking fumes. One boiling summer day she arrived in a fur coat with a swimsuit underneath so she could keep cool in the un-air-conditioned closet.

On many occasions Mario has said that clients want *him*, and by keeping his firm small, clients get him. He oversees every small detail personally, which, as one designer cattily commented, might take a job a little longer to complete, but on the other hand, there is little risk that the client's expectations of a Buatta room won't be met.

"I function very well in chaos. I hate empty spaces," the designer has remarked, and it can be believed by anyone who has seen his office. Speaking on several phones at once and exemplifying the concept of multitasking, he is able to accomplish so much by blurring the line between his personal and business life.

OPPOSITE *In 1983 a miniature version of one of Mario's show-house rooms, executed by designer Edward Acevedo, was displayed in one of the Fifth Avenue windows of Tiffany & Co.*

$1.50 • SEPTEMBER 5, 1983

INCLUDING CUE
MOVIES • TV • THEATER • RESTAURANTS

FOREVER YOUNG

The Saga of Peter Ivers • By Tony Schwartz

NEW YORK

The Status Merchants

Guaranteeing the Right Look • By Joan Kron

From the New Book 'Home-Psych'

The Buatta Look

A Mario Buatta room is instantly recognizable. *House & Garden*'s 1970 caption for his own living room could describe many of the hundreds of rooms he has created since: "Glazed walls; the English country look; porcelain hung as art; dark, dark floors; straw basketry; lacquer; potted flowers; table-top still life." While some have asserted that his rooms all look the same, this can be attributed in part to his clients' proclivity for the Buatta signature style as well as by intention. Mario explained to *Interview* magazine, "I believe in saturation—an old advertising stunt. Through saturation the look becomes indelible, and thus memorable. People have laughed at me over the years, but the same people are now hanging pictures from sashes and bows, and using chintzes like there's no tomorrow."

When Mario's rooms were first seen, they caused comment for their opulence and elegance. They were traditional, but an exuberant color palette and riot of pattern served up a novel, fresh prettiness. In the 1980s, Mario was one of the most well-known decorators in the country, if not *the* most. His look resonated with the times of new big money interested in acquiring an instant established backdrop. This was the essence of the English-country-house style, and Mario, along with his imitators, protégés, and rivals, was able to supply it. Mario early on revealed his awareness of his clients' motives to the magazine *Connoisseur*: "When they come to me I give them a sort of Instant Heritage look! It sounds vile, but for some clients it makes sense. It gives them a facade to hide behind."

Mario's work builds on the legacy of John Fowler, who along with his design partner, Nancy Lancaster, has been credited as the inventor of the English-country-house style. This style was a romanticized vision of what an English stately home should look like, but was much more comfortable and colorful than the natural occurring specimen. From first laying eyes on Nancy Lancaster's yellow room and from studying Fowler's work firsthand alongside its creator, Mario learned the style's language and absorbed its nuances. However, the raw materials Fowler had to work with were not the same as what Mario found back in the States.

Whereas John Fowler designed mostly for sprawling stately homes and Georgian townhouses, Mario recalibrated the look for apartment living and adjusted the proportions and scale accordingly. It is not uncommon for him to forbid an eight-inch bullion fringe for an ottoman because one's ceilings aren't high enough. Bringing classical order and balance to these rooms was an essential first step to achieving the style.

Mario acquired a formidable understanding of a room's architectural requirements, and he has often moved doors, put in correctly scaled ceiling cornices, and implemented other modifications to a room's hardscape to make it work. The Mariah Carey project is only one example that illustrates this. A loftlike space with no detail to speak of was completely laid out and fitted with Deco-style moldings and a coffered ceiling that suited the building's period and the cinematic glamour requested by the client. While not often photographed, his bathrooms are notable for both their suitability and great style, such as the zigzag Moderne mirrored one for a client in the Sherry-Netherland Hotel.

Both Mario and Fowler are celebrated for their elaborate dressmaker curtains that are always lined, interlined, and trimmed. It is not a love of frippery and frills that is responsible for this penchant. Rather, there's an understanding that curtains are the final enhancement of a room's architecture and that their design should follow the room's pretensions so that the more formal the room, the more elaborate the draperies, replete with valance, trimmings, and other embellishments. It harkens to the idea of suitability as described by Edith Wharton and Ogden Codman, Jr. in their 1897 book *The Decoration of Houses*.

OPPOSITE *When Mario showed John Fowler the photographs of his apartment in* House & Garden, *Fowler accused Mario of copying him. Mario rebutted that it wasn't a copy, but his own interpretation.*

Another signature element of the style is to affect the look of multigenerational accumulation. This is achieved with masses of collections, pictures hung in different ways, and an array of fabrics for the seat coverings, including slipcovers, which were historically used to protect costly silk damasks and velvets and nowadays give that offhand, lived-in atmosphere inherent to the look. Mario has said, "John could make a room look natural, as though it had always been just the way he planned it. He had a knack of knowing when to stop. You have to know what 'more' is in order to appreciate 'less.'"

Fowler was fabled for his color sense and sure hand with luminous oyster grays, pinks, and piquant yellows. He once gave Mario a yellow paint chip from Avery Row, but it, like many of his other colors, didn't have the same quality in North American light as it did in English. Mario developed his own palette of clear colors and is similarly celebrated for his color genius. Stanley Barrows, who urged Mario and others to look at the Post-Impressionist painters, applauded him for "his understanding of the use of fresh, sparkling color." While a Fowler coloration melts together like a Turner painting of Venice, Mario's dazzles like a Bonnard. His technique—covering walls with canvas that is applied with several layers of paint and glaze over a month-long period—imbues a room with a color-soaked incandescence.

Besides colors that please, whimsy and wit counterbalance the architectural formality. Colefax and Fowler had the artist George Oakes to achieve various trompe-l'oeil and other painted decoration, and Mario turned to Robert Jackson, who conjured up trellis floors, latticework ceilings, and woodland entry halls. Jackson began his career in London, where he worked on the 1960s restoration of Horace Walpole's "Goth-ick" villa Strawberry Hill before moving to New York in 1965 to work with Sister Parish, and was perfectly equipped to realize Mario's romantic visions.

Another lesson learned from Fowler was to incorporate humble or rustic elements to keep a room from skewing too fancy. Mario recalls, "He said if you get grand on one thing, play it down on the next three things." An example of this tenet is using chintz, a printed cotton, rather than a more formal fabric. Fabric purveyor Christopher Hyland, who honored Mario with a Hyland Award for Excellence in Design in 2012, notes, "Buatta has employed lively printed floral chintzes to great advantage. They are his foil, his guarantee that no room orchestrated by his aesthetic genius will be rendered stiff, formalistic, or staid. Buatta employs them with purpose, as emissaries of joyful design." Mario's current living room, which is glazed pistachio green and lavishly layered with paintings and porcelains, is offset by a bare wood floor painted to resemble sisal. Just as Mario has commented that John Fowler's work for the National Trust never became "museum-y," in essence lifeless, like pinned insects, Mario's rooms are instilled with a spontaneity.

"People have laughed at me over the years, but the same people are now hanging pictures from sashes and bows, and using chintzes like there's no tomorrow."
— MARIO BUATTA

For a Barneys New York window in 2000, Creative Director Simon Doonan selected Mario and his penchant for chintz to epitomize the 1980s and the era's conspicuous consumption. Everything, from the crown molding to the soles of the live models' shoes, was covered in yellow-ground Floral Bouquet chintz.

Mario's rooms are always cited for their comfort. The voluptuousness of form, size, and overstuffedness of his soft upholstery is one of his signatures. Upholsterer Ken DeAngelis explains how Shar Pei-like wrinkles are purposely left where the muslin stretches over down so that a deep plushness is readily apparent to the eye. However, as former assistant Beth Martell observes, Mario created comfort not just with plush upholstery but also visually with gorgeous color compositions, and even olfactorily, as he often recommends scenting the air with pomander balls or a sachet of potpourri behind seat cushions to envelope the sitter.

Just as Fowler's work influenced Mario, Mario himself has influenced legions of design professionals and enthusiasts. In addition to earning dozens of accolades, awards, and honorary doctorates, The New York School of Interior Design named their materials library The Mario Buatta Materials Atelier (jokingly called the I-telier by the designer "because I'm I-talian") in 2011. The school's president, David Sprouls, noted, "The atelier is a beautiful light-filled place where students gather, work, and learn amongst a vast selection of material samples. Naming it after Mario Buatta, a legend so identified with his masterful use of fabric and color, imbues the space with richer meaning, inspiring the next generation of designers."

The Mario Buatta look has come to define an era in American culture as ebullient and luxuriant as the beauty of his rooms. Journalist John Taylor wrote in 1986 that Mario was "the most voluptuous, the most emotional of the English-country-house style [practitioners]," and it is this esprit that even his most talented imitators aren't able to copy. The pendulum of fashion swings back and forth, but Mario has always been secure knowing that beauty and comfort never go out of style.

Emily Evans Eerdmans
New York City

"The Prince of Chintz Song"
(excerpt)

To the tune of "'O Sole Mio"

As a bambino he seemed to know,
While still in diapers he hated Art Deco!
His family's house was white and chrome
He cried, "If this décor stays, I'm-a leaving home!"

His dear Aunt Mary, his Auntie Mame,
She praised his talent, his path to fame;
He loved strong colors, Mama was nonplussed,
Her son loved chintz and welcomed dust!

Written by Christopher Mason

OPPOSITE *Winning the ultimate sign of icon status,*
Mario was the subject of an Absolut vodka advertisement that featured
an Absolut bottle filled with Mario's potpourri and topped with
a pleated and pinked lampshade in one of his fabrics.

ABSOLUT BUATTA.

*Clockwise from top left: the geranium
pink entrance hall with faux-marble
pilasters; the forty-foot-long
grapefruit yellow living room with
brown satin curtains at the windows
and white upholstery throughout;
the library covered in antique Chinese
paper; the soft olive green-stained
paneled dining room is accented
with pink-covered Queen Anne side
chairs and floral porcelain displayed
in the two niches; the card room,
painted green faux-tortoiseshell by
Robert Jackson with brass trim, is a
riff on Albert Hadley's famous library
for Mrs. Vincent Astor. Its ceiling
is covered in silver tea paper to add
shimmer and luxe.*

Postscript

I call this project "Unfinished Dream" because it was never
completed. Just as the curtains were being hung, the owners
decided to move abroad. I always say a room should grow
over time like a garden. These rooms are seedlings.

Mario Buatta

426

SELECT BIBLIOGRAPHY

Alsop, Susan Mary. "Blair House." *Architectural Digest* (October 1988): 164–177, 264.

Amaya, Mario. "Mario Buatta." *Interview* (March 1986): 129–130.

Aronson, Steven M.L. "A house of many hues." *Architectural Digest* (March 2009): 74–83.

_____. "A Virginia thoroughbred." *Architectural Digest* (December 2003): 168–175, 248.

"The art of the interior." *Architectural Digest* (September 2001): 92.

Bancroft, Barbara. "Mario Buatta: living legend." *Quest* (Summer 2006): 104–109.

Bedell, Geraldine. "Made in the USA." *The Sunday Times* (London) (August 12, 1990): section 7, 1.

Bernikow, Louise. "Castles, manors and halls—an English pilgrimage." *Architectural Digest* (June 1985): 296.

Bethany, Marilyn. "America the Buatta-ful." *New York* (March, 27, 1989): 62–63.

_____. "Mario the epicurean." *New York* (April 18, 1988): 76.

_____. "What works: priceless tips from the super-decorators." *New York* (April 13, 1987): 36.

Bissell, Therese. "Romancing history." *Architectural Digest* (December 2006): 160–169, 221.

Boodro, Michael. "All hail the Prince of Chintz! Mario Buatta interior designer." *House Beautiful* (June 2002): 61–66.

"Brownstone with a Southwest accent." *New York Times Magazine* (September 26, 1971).

Buatta, Mario. "Designer postcards." *House & Garden* (April 1988): 52.

_____. "Mario Buatta on John Fowler's Hunting Lodge." *Architectural Digest* (January 2003): 109.

Buckley, Christopher. "Malcolm Forbes at Timberfield." *Architectural Digest* (March 1988): 92–99.

Byrd, Mary. "The world of Mario Buatta." *Architectural Digest* (June 1982): 208–212.

Carlsen, Peter. "The lingering past." *Architectural Digest* (March 1985): 150–155.

_____. "Savoir faire." *Architectural Digest* (September 1984): 90–99.

Cheever, Susan. "Mario Buatta: a lifetime's collections define a New York apartment." *Architectural Digest* (September 1997): 158.

Clark, Sally. "Today's romantic bedrooms." *House Beautiful* (April 1991): 54–57.

Clarke, Gerald. "*Architectural Digest* visits Mariah Carey." *Architectural Digest* (November 2001): 244–251.

_____. "Serenity found on Biscayne Bay." *Architectural Digest* (April 2006): 172–179.

_____. "The view from the top." *Architectural Digest* (November 2005): 204–211, 281.

Collier's Yearbook 1971. London: Crowell-Collier Educational Corp., 1971.

Collins, Nancy. "A dash of dazzle on Fifth." *Architectural Digest* (February 2008): 158–166.

_____. "Luxury, Texas style." *Architectural Digest* (July 2007): 64–73.

"Color bloom in a vintage farmhouse." *House Beautiful's Home Decorating* (Winter 1979–80): 66–71.

Craig, David Cobb. "Connecting to Collecting." *Art and Antique Dealers League of America Spring Show NYC Guide* (May 2013): 8–13.

Cropper, Carol Marie. "Dog art." *Forbes* (October 12, 1992): 148–149.

"Designer secrets: Mario Buatta." *Architectural Digest* (January 2006): 42–45.

Driemen, John. "A colorful character." *Art & Antiques* (September 1998): 56–61.

Drucker, Stephen. "No place like home." *Architectural Digest* (April 2003): 224–233.

Duka, John. "Duka's diary." *House & Garden* (March 1988): 226.

Dwyer, Michael Middleton. *Carolands*. San Mateo, CA: San Mateo County Historical Association, 2006.

Eerdmans, Emily Evans. "Master class." *House Beautiful* (October 2012): 38.

"Everything in its place." *House & Garden* (January 1981): 120–121.

Ferreri, James G. "It's good to be the prince." *Staten Island Advance* (September 26, 2002): D1.

Finch, Christopher. "Personalized portraits: Jeremiah's renderings of great rooms." *Architectural Digest* (February 2002): 82–94.

"40 decorating ideas to make the most of your house." *House & Garden* (January 1970): 56–57.

Frank, Michael. "One part inspiration." *Architectural Digest* (August 2006): 116–123, 180.

"Garden-green room, flower-garden patterns." *House & Garden* (May 1975): 90–95.

"The Georgian mode in modern dress." *Architectural Digest* (May/June 1976): 70–73.

Gaynor, Elizabeth, ed. "Winning combinations." *House & Garden* (April 1982): 64.

Goldberger, Paul. "Rural revisited." *Architectural Digest* (May 1994): 112–121, 202.

Goodman, Mark S. "Designing the dollar." *Money* (November 1986): 112.

Greene, Elaine. "A New York of one's own." *Architectural Digest* (April 1987): 204–209.

Greenfield-Sanders, Timothy. "Giants of design." *House Beautiful* (June 2002): 60–188.

_____. "Color feast." *House & Garden* (June 1985): 164–169.

Grundy, Lester and Jack Macurdy, eds. "For that most special day." *House Beautiful* (December 1975): 64–65.

"Halls into rooms." *House & Garden* (February 1971): 76.

Harrell, Glenn. "The Buatta bedroom." *House Beautiful* (June 1990): 78–81.

"*HB* designer room." *House Beautiful* (September 1978): 120–121.

"Head of the table." *Avenue* (May 2011): 76–79.

Heck, Marlene Elizabeth. *Blair House: the president's guest house*. Charlottesville, VA: Thomasson-Grant, 1989.

Heilpern, John. "My glorious, nosebleeding night as a god." *The New York Observer* (November 30, 1992).

Holtzman, Joseph, ed. "Mario Buatta in the living room." *Nest: a quarterly of interiors* (Summer 2001): 70–93.

House & Garden editors. *House & Garden's best in decoration*. New York: Condé Nast Publications, 1987.

"A house of your ideas." *House & Garden* (August 1978): 100–107.

"How color pulls a room together." *House & Garden* (March 1976): 88–89.

"How to make your room come alive with color." *House & Garden* (March 1975): 44–47.

Howell, Georgina. "American greats." *House & Garden* (September 1988): 140–159, 243.

"Impressionistic look for décor." *Architectural Digest* (May/June 1974): 24.

Jackson, Paula Rice. "On the cover." *House & Garden* (November 1980): 12.

_____. "Mario the impresario." *Spotlight* (April 1988): 28–33, 66.

Kennedy, Margaret. "Is pretty dead?" *House Beautiful* (September 1998): 64.

Kontos, Jason. "Blue and white porcelain—the all-time favorite collection." *House Beautiful* (February 1982): 70–71.

Kornbluth, Jesse. "Manhattan romance." *Architectural Digest* (February 1997): 100–107.

Lopez-Córdero, Mario. "Mario Buatta." *New York* (October 29, 2007): 94–99.

Macurdy, Jack, ed. "5 Statements with Style." *House Beautiful* (January 1977): 56–65.

Malone, Maggie. "Decorators making furniture." *Newsweek* (April 10 1989): 72.

Margolies, Jane. "English country, made for today." *House Beautiful* (May 1989): 58–63.

"Mario Buatta." *Architectural Digest: The AD 100, an exclusive guide to the world's finest interior designers* (August 15, 1990): 60–62.

"Mario Buatta." *Metropolitan Home* (February 1989): 140–144.

Mason, Christopher. "Master of ceremonies." *Architectural Digest* (July 2013): 136–147.

Mehle, Aileen. "Charlotte Ford's Southampton." *Architectural Digest* (May 1992): 120–127.

_____. "Continental calm on high." *Architectural Digest* (November 1989): 220–227.

_____. "East coast English." *Architectural Digest* (November 2004): 212–221.

_____. "A New York story." *Architectural Digest* (February 1999): 150–159, 238.

_____. "Southampton statement." *Architectural Digest* (May 2001): 194–201, 254.

_____. "Shall we dance?" *Architectural Digest* (January 2012): 188–195.

"Mr. Peeper's nights: carrying on." *New York* (January 28 1991): 12–13.

"Mr. Peeper's nights: far out in Far Hills." *New York* (January 28 1985): 33–34.

Mortimer, Senga. "Jewels of design." *House Beautiful* (February 2003): 88–97.

"National treasures: new reproductions from Winterthur." *House & Garden* (October 1982): 74–79.

Norwich, William. "Delicate arrangements." *House & Garden* (April 1998): 168–175.

"On the cover." *House & Garden* (February 1982): 2.

"On the cover." *New York Times Magazine* (October 1, 1972): Section 6, Part 2.

Owens, Mitchell. "At long last love." *New York Times Magazine* (Spring 2001).

"Patterned around porcelain." *House Beautiful* (October 1978): 10–11.

Perschetz, Lois. "Analysis of a stylish bedroom." *House Beautiful* (August 1984): 43–47, 113–14.

Pittell, Christine. "Kips Bay show house 2006." *House Beautiful* (August 2006): 72–75.

_____. "25 years of Kips Bay." *House Beautiful* (September 1997): 122–123.

Plaskin, Glenn. "Mario Buatta touches up the joint." *Daily News* (New York, NY) magazine (October 8, l989): 18–19, 30, 32.

"Polished and pretty." *House & Garden* (February 1983): 104–109.

"Pretty treatments for windows." *House & Garden* (January 1971): 80–81.

Prisant, Carol. "Show and tell." *House Beautiful* (November 2000): 166–170.

"Regal grace." *House Beautiful* (November 1977): 130–133.

"Revitalizing beds in relaxing bedrooms." *House & Garden* (August 1975): 50–51.

Simpson, Jeffrey. "*AD* Travels: Connecticut connections." *Architectural Digest* (September 1994): 26–45.

Skurka, Norma. "To coddle the ego." *New York Times Magazine* (December 19, 1971): 40.

Skurka, Norma. *The New York Times Book of Interior Design and Decoration.* New York: Times Books, 1976.

Slesin, Suzanne. "When chintz meets steel." *House & Garden* (May 1998): 144–149.

"Style makers today." *House Beautiful* (November 1986): 66–79.

Tapert, Annette. "English tailoring for Park Avenue." *Architectural Digest* (October 1999): 214–223, 304.

_____. "Mario Buatta." *Architectural Digest* (January 2001): 122–129.

Taylor, John. "Fringe lunatic." *Manhattan,inc.* (July 1986).

Thomas, Michael M. "Refined continuity." *Architectural Digest* (December 1985): 178–181, 198.

"Timeless rooms." *House & Garden* (March 1993): 186.

Tolleson, Katrin, ed. "The touch of a master decorator." *House Beautiful* (January 1984): 48–55.

Tolleson, Katrin and Carolyn Englefield-Carter, ed. "English country style." *House Beautiful* (November 1985): 57–63.

"Travel notes: Mario Buatta." *Architectural Digest* (June 1985): 296–306.

Vaill, Amanda. "A colorful embrace." *Architectural Digest* (December 2009): 114–123.

Vogel, Carol. "Home design: in the Baldwin tradition." *New York Times Magazine* (May 3, 1987): 91.

_____. "A living scrapbook." *New York Times Magazine* (September 6 1987): 34–37.

_____. "New vitality." *Architectural Digest* (May 1980): 76–83.

von Hoffman, Nicholas. "Mario Buatta." *Architectural Digest* (February 2002): 60–62.

Walker, Michael. "But was the $18,000 curtain beautiful?" *Spy Magazine* (October 1989): 100–112.

"Waking up the bedroom." *House & Garden* (May 1981): 124–127.

Wasserstein, Wendy. "The Mario chronicles." *House & Garden* (May 1991): 76.

Weston, Marybeth and Margaret McQuade. "Creating high standards." *House & Garden* (January 1981): 82–83.

"Where every room opens up a whole new view of color." *House & Garden* (March 1980): 122–127.

Winkel, Gabrielle. "Anglo-American tradition." *House & Garden* (May 1986): 144–151.

_____. "Englishing a brownstone." *House & Garden* (October 1984): 190–197.

"Wood + color = warmth." *House & Garden* (September 1980): 124–125.

"The world according to ... Mario Buatta." *Avenue* (January 2012): 96.

ACKNOWLEDGMENTS

I'd first like to thank my alter ego, Mario Buatta, whose head has never left my shoulders, guiding me through this varied career of fifty years. This book would not have been possible without the following people: Paige Rense, editor emeritus of *Architectural Digest*, who wrote the foreword; Emily Evans Eerdmans for her patience and fortitude while translating my thoughts and dreams onto the page, and Maureen Footer for introducing me to Emily; Charles Miers, my publisher at Rizzoli, for his perseverance in convincing me to do this book; Philip Reeser, my editor, for his patience throughout the process; Anthony Petrillose for early guidance; Richard Pandiscio and Bill Loccisano for designing the book I always imagined; Donald and Si Newhouse for their generosity and belief in my career; Margaret Russell, editor-in-chief of *Architectural Digest*, and her staff, particularly Mitchell Owens and Howard Christian; the outstanding team at Condé Nast Publications, including Leigh Montville, Marianne Brown, Lindsay Foster, Cynthia Cathcart, Stan Friedman, and Deirdre McCabe Nolan; from Brunschwig & Fils, Brigitta Williamson, who has always generously contributed to my show-house rooms, and Cary Kravet for the Spatterware wallpaper that graces the cover; Christopher Mason for lending his clever and amusing lyrics; Christopher Hyland for his erudite insights; my brother, Joseph, who helped provide family photographs; the late Wendy Wasserstein for her friendship and whose great humor is found herein; Karen Lerman, Sarah Heinemann, and James Abrew at Kravet for their kind assistance with photos; and Patricia Altschul, Alice Diamond, Chippy Irvine, Aileen Mehle, Hilary and Wilbur Ross, and from Colefax and Fowler, design director George Oakes and archivist Barrie McIntyre for their special contributions to this book. Special thanks to Apple Parish Bartlett and Susan Bartlett Crater for the quotation from their book *Sister: The Life of Legendary Interior Decorator Mrs. Henry Parish II*.

There have been many people who have inspired, guided, and supported me: Albert Hadley who recommended I take Parsons European Summer Session with Professor Stanley Barrows, which changed my life and opened my eyes to a world of interior decoration; John Fowler for his ultimate inspiration; Mary Jane Pool who published my first show-house room in *House & Garden* in 1969 and Norma Skurka who published my second show-house room on the cover of the *The Home* magazine of the *New York Times*; Joanne Creveling, Harriet Weintraub, Marilyn Evins, and Marilyn White who were my comrades-in-arms at the Winter Antiques Show; the talented Jeremiah Goodman for his illustrations; the late Clement E. Conger for asking me to decorate Blair House, the White House's guest quarters; Ann and Charles Johnson for the experience of working with them on their historic chateau Carolands; the artist Robert Jackson and his talented staff; Morton Hamburg for his friendship and sage advice; the late Helen Hollerith who selected me as one of the designers for the first Kips Bay Show House of 1973 and Diantha Nype, Kips Bay's publicity dynamo.

Deep appreciation goes to all the people who believed in me and captured my work in words and pictures, including Lemeau Arrott-Watt, Joann Barwick, Julie Baumgold (also known as Mr. Peepers), Marilyn Bethany, Michael Boodro, Erica Brown, Michael Bruno, Dara Caponigro, Graydon Carter, Richard Champion, Heather Cohane, Charles Cohen, David Patrick Columbia, Kendell Cronstrom, Bill Cunningham, Billy Cunningham, Julie Dannenberg, Peter Davis, Barbaralee Diamonstein, Carrie Donovan, Stephen Drucker, Feliciano, Scott Frances, Carolyn Englefield, Ralph Gardner Jr., Jacqueline Gonnet, Wendy Goodman, Kaaren Parker Gray, Penelope Green, Elaine Greene, Louis Oliver Gropp, Mick Hales, Lizzie Himmel, Jeffrey Hirsch, Joseph Holtzman, Chauncey Howell, James Huntington, Paula Rice Jackson, Thibault Jeanson, Nick Johnson, Peggy Kennedy, Jura Koncius, Jason Kontos, Joan Kron, George Lange, Debra Lex, Chris Casson Madden, Ann Maine, Marian McEvoy, Monica Meenan, Senga Mortimer, Enid Nemy, Nancy Newhouse, Billy Norwich, Nancy Novograd, Frances Pellegrini, Eric Piasecki, Christine Pittel, Glenn Plaskin, Carol Prisant, Marianne Rohrlich, Dan Shaw, Doris Shaw, Jeffrey Simpson, Suzy Slesin, Liz Smith, Carolyn Sollis, Tony Soluri, André Leon Talley, John Taylor, Newell Turner, Charlyne Varkonyi, Pilar Viladas, Carol Vogel, Anna Wintour, Sander Witlin, Bruce Wolf, and Sandra Zummo.

To Christopher Maya, the very talented designer who made an early decision to not accept employment, and to so many others who did accept (and lived to regret it!), I give my thanks for their nerve, courage, and much appreciated help. Many have gone on to achieve success in a tough business, and I congratulate them.

And, finally, to all my clients who have put up with me these many years; all the artisans, craftsmen, and tradespeople who have made my work possible; and all those friends and colleagues whom I inadvertently omitted, I thank you deeply for fifty—and counting—wonderful years.

Mario Buatta

IMAGE CREDITS

Clockwise from top center: "More victims of the Velcro wall paneling scam" postcard; bewigged with House Beautiful *editor Joann Barwick; with Wendy Wasserstein at Mario's 60th birthday party; "Set the hour and I'll TURNUP" postcard; Mario sporting new Billy Bob teeth; Enid Nemy seated on a chintz sofa at Judy Green's 60th birthday party celebration for Mario— Christopher Mason later sang "Don't put that chintz upon the chair, little Mario" to the tune of a Noël Coward song; lampshaded for a party held in honor of Aileen Mehle at the Plaza; Anne Eisenhower; a woman and her master at the hairdresser.*

THE
MARIO BUATTA
COLLECTION

Mario Buatta

JOHN WIDDICOMB
COMPANY

Greetings
FROM

THE HO

First published in the United States of America in 2013 by
Rizzoli International Publications, Inc.
300 Park Avenue South
New York, NY 10010
www.rizzoliusa.com

© 2013 Mario Buatta

Editor: Philip Reeser
Design: Mario Buatta, Richard Pandiscio, William Loccisano / Pandiscio Co.
Production: Colin Hough-Trapp

2021 2022 / 10 9 8 7 6 5 4

Distributed in the U.S. trade by Random House, New York

Printed in China

ISBN-13: 978-0-8478-4072-4

Library of Congress Catalog Control Number: 2013939683

"The Prince of Chintz Song"
(excerpt)

To the tune of "America the Beautiful"

Oh Buatta-ful for swags and swirls,
Chinoiserie and chintz;
For lime-green walls
And topiary balls,
Styled as befits a prince;
Terrific and prolific,
He's a legend in our time;
Too bad he's kind of crazy,
But his work is quite sublime.

Written by Christopher Mason